Praise for *Why Should Anyone Buy From You?*

D1416775

❚❚ Justin lays it out straight. Putting social purpose and humanity back into the heart of commercial enterprise is an idea whose time has come. Trust is not just a pre-requisite for doing good business, but is the fundamental bedrock of a sustainable society. This book is for anyone that believes we can do much better. Read it, reflect on it and then get straight out there and do something about it.
TOM FARRAND, CO-FOUNDER OF THE PIPELINE PROJECT AND GOOD FOR NOTHING

❚❚ Winning the trust of the consumer is increasingly difficult in many of today's cynical and challenging markets. Commitment, longevity, insight, art and science all need to be brought into play to successfully build trust. Justin engagingly and practically explores these themes and how they can impact your business in a must-read for anyone wanting to build a trusted brand.
FARAH RAMZAN GOLANT, CHAIRMAN, ABBOTT MEAD VICKERS

Why Should Anyone Buy From You?

FT Prentice Hall
FINANCIAL TIMES

In an increasingly competitive world, we believe it's quality of
thinking that gives you the edge – an idea that opens new
doors, a technique that solves a problem or an insight that
simply makes sense of it all. The more you know, the smarter
and faster you can go.

That's why we work with the best minds in business and finance
to bring cutting-edge thinking and best learning practice to a
global market.

Under a range of leading imprints, including *Financial Times
Prentice Hall*, we create world-class print publications and
electronic products bringing our readers knowledge, skills and
understanding, that can be applied whether studying or at work.

To find out more about Pearson Education publications, or tell us
about the books you'd like to find, you can visit us at
www.pearson.com/uk

PEARSON

Why Should Anyone Buy From You?

Earn customer trust to
drive business success

Justin Basini

Financial Times
Prentice Hall
is an imprint of

Harlow, England • London • New York • Boston • San Francisco • Toronto
Sydney • Tokyo • Singapore • Hong Kong • Seoul • Taipei • New Delhi
Cape Town • Madrid • Mexico City • Amsterdam • Munich • Paris • Milan

PEARSON EDUCATION LIMITED

Edinburgh Gate
Harlow CM20 2JE
Tel: +44 (0)1279 623623
Fax: +44 (0)1279 431059
Website: www.pearson.com/uk

First published in Great Britain in 2011

Pearson Education is not responsible for the content of third-party Internet sites.

ISBN: 978-0-273-74551-8

British Library Cataloguing-in-Publication Data
A catalogue record for this book is available from the British Library

Library of Congress Cataloging-in-Publication Data
Basini, Justin.
  Why should anyone buy from you? : earn customer trust to drive business success
/ Justin Basini. -- 1st ed.
      p. cm.
  Includes bibliographical references and index.
  ISBN 978-0-273-74551-8 (pbk.)
  1. Selling. 2. Customer relations. 3. Trust. I. Title.
  HF5438.25.B377 2011
  658.85--dc23
                              2011021975

10 9 8 7 6 5 4 3 2 1
15 14 13 12 11

Text design by Design Deluxe
Shopping bag image by LiveSurface Image Library

Typeset in 11/15pt Myriad Pro Regular by 3
Printed and bound in Great Britain by Ashford Colour Press Ltd., Gosport

To Victoria who, every day, shows me how to love and trust

Contents

Acknowledgements

My legs turned to jelly and I threw up as I entered the tunnel on the Embankment in London, just as you go under Blackfriars Bridge. The road was littered with vomit, urine, empty water bottles and a few bodies, either lying prostrate or leaning against the walls, desperately trying to get a break from the pain. I was stripped bare of all my belief and resolve. Despite having come so far, I couldn't go on.

The dark, dank recesses of this bridge were a private hell which I was sharing with hundreds of others. People streamed past, some looking healthy, some looking awful – each individual enduring their own test of brain over body.

I looked up and saw the brightness ahead of me, the crowds, the river of humanity battling through sweat and tears to achieve a goal. I steadied myself for the last push. Gently, tentatively, I stretched my over-used legs – every movement was excruciating. One leaden foot in front of another, I started the final push to the end. As I gathered pace, I left the darkness behind and was warmed by the rays of the sun and cheers of the crowd lining the banks of the River Thames, seemingly imploring me individually to go on to glory.

Every step of that last one and half miles through Parliament Square, St James's Park and the Mall to the end of the 2006 London Marathon was exhausted pain. Even as I could see the finish it didn't get any easier. I never got a second wind, a final burst of energy – it was just me, my feet, my brain and a goal.

Writing this book has been like the two London marathons I've run. Hours and hours spent in service of a difficult achievement. I hoped that I would get better at writing and find it easier as I went on through this project, but it didn't turn out that way; it was just a hard slog.

That slog was only made easier because it was shared.

Thanks go first to Jon Elek, my agent at AP Watt, without whom this project would never have got off the ground, and to Stephen King, who introduced us. Stephen, a voracious consumer of business books and ideas, reviewed the manuscript and gave many fantastic examples and comments. The team at Pearson – most notably Liz Gooster, my publisher – believed in me and my ideas while encouraging me to broaden my scope into business and resist my more academic tendencies!

Thanks, next, to my many friends and mentors who gave their time in interviews: Bill McDonald, Cathryn Sleight, Chris Satterthwaite, Cilla Snowball, Lord David Currie, Farah Ramzan Golant, Fr Jack Maloney, Dr Marek Kohn, Mark Ritson, Mike Hughes, Robin Wight, Rory Sutherland, Srini Gopalan and Tom Farrand. They helped shape many of the ideas in the book and they should take the credit that this deserves.

Big thanks to Dominic Grounsell, too, who pointed me in the right direction many times as he read the manuscript. Also, to his team at Capital One, many of whom used to work with me, for allowing me to road test some of the ideas with them.

If you've been educated by the Jesuits, as I have, they always get a look in and, specifically, I would like to extend my thanks to Fr Jack Maloney SJ, who helped me rethink the balance and creative purpose of business, and Fr Michael Holman SJ, who put me on to the idea of virtue and Tom Wright's thinking.

I also wish to thank the Carmelite Community in Quidenham, Norfolk, of which my aunt, Sr Maria Basini, is a member, for hiding me away in the seclusion and quiet of their monastery to finish the manuscript.

My mum, dad and sister deserve huge thanks for supporting and encouraging me over the years, even when they didn't have a clue what I was doing or why.

Finally, and most importantly, immense thanks are due to my family, who bear the brunt of the pain as I progress my projects. My wife, Victoria, who selflessly puts her life and career on hold to care for and love me and our family, and to my three children, Luca, Daniel and Jemima, who have to put up with an irascible and moody thinker as a dad. Truly, this book was brought to you by team Basini. We hope you get value from it.

Justin Basini

Publisher's acknowledgements

We are grateful to the following for permission to reproduce copyright material:

Figure 2.2 from IPSOS MORI, 'Trust in the Professions' survey, 1993-2009, 'Who do we trust and how is it changing?'; Figure 2.3 from 2010 Edelman Global Trust Barometer survey – How much do you trust business to do what's right?; Figure 2.4 from TrustR brand by country survey by Millward Brown. TrustR is a special analysis from BrandZ, the Global brand equity study invented and run by Millward Brown for WPP; Figure 2.5 from *The Brand Bubble*, Jossey-Bass (Gerzema, J. and Lebar, E. 2008).

In some instances we have been unable to trace the owners of copyright material, and we would appreciate any information that would enable us to do so.

Introduction

WHY TRUST MAKES YOU MONEY

Trust is the bedrock of the economy, your business and your brand. Without trust, your interactions with your customers, your suppliers, the media, the regulator, your colleagues, even your boss, become impossibly difficult and expensive. Win trust and you can turbo-charge your success, but the question is, how? People are more cynical, more empowered and less trusting than ever before, but you can learn how to create a trusted business and brand.

What are you doing right now?

Are you in a bookshop, browsing in your lunch break or on your way home after a hard day? Perhaps you are in an airport, looking for a distraction for a few hours as you jet off. Are you at your computer, browsing through the pages of Amazon?

Now try a thought experiment. Imagine your day without the trust you place in people, things and your own experiences. Could you handle the complex myriad of decisions you make, big and small, without trust?

Would you have eaten that bowl of cereal if you couldn't trust what was in it?

Would you have got in that train or car if you didn't trust its mechanics?

Will you get on that plane without trusting in the ground staff, the fuel, the plane itself, the pilot or even your fellow passengers?

Do you believe your partner when he or she says, 'I love you?'

It may be obvious, but trust is a vital ingredient in all of our daily lives. We are programmed, through our very physiology, our psychology and our life experiences, to trust. Trust makes our lives so much easier that, without it, the sheer effort of living would become far too great. People with larger networks of trusting friends and family live longer and are healthier. Despite what our somewhat cynical age might have us believe, to trust is far from naïve, but a skill learned, refined and practised by the more intelligent.

Our economy and the markets they are built on rely on trust. When markets fail, as they have so painfully recently, it is generally because, somewhere, trust has failed. Every MBA student and economist in the world will have been asked to read Adam Smith's *An Inquiry into the Nature and Causes of the Wealth of Nations* (1776) – more commonly known as simply *The Wealth of Nations* (although how many read the whole work is questionable!) – but most will never read *The Theory of Moral Sentiments* – the book Smith published in 1759, 17 years before his more famous work. Smith knew that markets couldn't operate without a framework – a moral one in his mind – to create predictable and rational behaviour between market participants. In the language of the economist, trust reduces transaction costs, allowing commerce to happen.

All great businesses know that getting customers to trust them is vital if they are to sell their products or services. Marketers and brand-builders have long played the trust-building game to influence our decisions. From Josiah Wedgwood in 1772, placing his name on every piece of china he shipped, to BP today, reeling from their polluting disaster in the Gulf of Mexico, all are making promises and giving us signals about how much we can trust their quality, performance and value. Enron, Tyco,

Pepsi, Coca-Cola, Facebook, Google, BP and Toyota are just some of the businesses that have suffered crises in trust, often wiping billions from their stock market valuations or even causing their collapse.

We forget trust at our peril

Despite the essential nature of trust to our society, economy and well-being as individuals, it is easy to forget and perhaps take for granted. It is only when our faith in something is shaken or we are placed in an unfamiliar environment that we suddenly wake up to the possibility our decisions to trust might be wrong – or, at least, worth a second look.

In the developed world, product quality and performance is generally so high nowadays and the systems to ensure safety so advanced, that rarely do we question whether or not we should trust. Yet, go to a foreign country – especially a developing one – and look at the shelves and you will find yourself searching for those signals of a recognised brand or corporation in which to trust as you more consciously evaluate your purchases. Those signals are helping you decide whether or not the beer you are drinking, the cereal you are eating or the washing powder you are using will harm you or have the desired effect.

We only need remember the feelings we had as we witnessed the global financial meltdown of the past few years to realise that, without trust, panic can set in. Thousands queuing outside Northern Rock in 2006 as the fear of its collapse gripped the UK or the forlorn Lehman Brothers employee with a cardboard box in her arms as she left the office to look for another job are painful examples of the serious impact that a collapse of trust can have on our lives. The recent and current examples are many, from Lehman Brothers to BP to Toyota to British politicians' expenses to global warming science – all have suffered from serious, sometimes catastrophic, collapses in trust. Without trust, life becomes significantly more difficult. Remove trust and we need more legal frameworks, more regulation and tighter controls on how businesses and individuals operate.

Collapsing trust

Collapsing trust seems to be a very modern malaise, exploded by the Internet, the 24-hour news cycle and the changing social landscape. From neighbours not knowing each other, all the way to Islamic terrorism, the past few years have been awash with stories, analysis and opinion on how trust is changing. The subject has deserved many magazine covers, from the *Harvard Business Review* to *Wired* magazine. Every business leader, politician and pundit seems to be proclaiming that trust needs to be rebuilt.

It is easy to believe that there is a crisis in trust. Any study of the data, of which there are lots, and almost none that is really good, shows trust is changing. Trust in business, bankers, politicians and journalists is low and declining, whereas trust in doctors, the police, even the Church is increasing.

The changing landscape of trust is a complex one, though, because it is embedded in a web of inputs and outputs. We have so much more information, knowledge and communications to deal with than in the past. Combine this with fundamental shifts in our capability to process complexity and changing attitudes to fear and risk and it is no wonder that trust is a dynamic, not a static, property.

What is really going on with trust?

Do we no longer trust our system, our leaders, our neighbours, even ourselves? If we really don't trust the banks, why do we leave our money in them? If we really don't trust our politicians or political system, then why do the majority of us in developed democracies continue to put crosses on little pieces of paper? How is the exponential rise in access to information, and each other, changing our decisions to trust? Are these challenges mainly global, national or local?

What I think is clear is that these questions have a profound effect on many aspects of life and especially on businesses and brands. Whether it is a financial institution trying to reclaim customers' loyalty or the leadership of Toyota dealing with a global belief that their cars are unsafe or you and your marketing team putting together the latest campaign to sell the latest proposition, all are intrinsically aiming to make an appeal for the customer to trust.

The understanding of trust in business, however, despite its seeming importance, is low. The way that trust is measured is poor, only scratching the surface as to what is really going on. Banks are a good example. According to the data, everyone distrusts and 'hates' bankers – they now rate lower than even politicians – the banking system has near collapsed and they continue to pay their executives extremely large bonuses, yet we use the banking system every day, depositing our salaries and savings, spending with our debit and credit cards. Why aren't we hiding our money under the mattress?

Clearly, the diagnosis that banks aren't trusted is incorrect. Our behaviours and actions manifestly demonstrate that, at some level, we *do* trust banks (or at least the banking system), despite all the evidence to the contrary, to be stable and perform its function. Of course, at another level, it is true to say that we *don't* trust banks or bankers and we certainly don't like them. There must be more to trust than meets the eye or is captured by a simple market research question.

Fortunately, there has been a huge amount of analysis and experimentation done into trust by psychologists and sociologists. They have many theories and models of trust, but the extension of these into the business world has been limited, apart from one or two notable examples. Part of the purpose of this book is to explain this thinking and reapply some of these models to brands and business in order to build a deeper understanding of how trust affects the decisions that people make in order to do business.

Trust and brands as a source of social capital

Trust is a powerful source of social capital, where social capital is those assets that exist in our societies and between people – a wealth of sorts, which can be put to work in the pursuit of goals. Social capital and trust-building on a societal level has a lot to do with the ability of people to come together in formal or informal groups that are bound by reciprocal relationships and codes of behaviour. Whether it is a church, a Rotary Club or a trade body, these bonds build trust that helps transactions flow. As we will discover, people and societies that have a greater reserve of and capability to create trust do better economically, especially in the application of capitalism and modern democracy. Why have America, Germany and Japan done so well in the post-war period? It's a lot to do with the high levels of trust and social capital they can employ in creating wealth.

Brands exist as a store of trust. The economic purpose of brands is to reduce transaction costs between buyer and seller. Instead of having to assess the attributes of the 150 different ways of washing my clothes, I can choose my normal brand that I trust will perform in the way it always has and is at a price that I believe represents reasonable value. A decision that could have taken half an hour, reduced to seconds. Brands are a convenient way to make choices in our crowded world and even more overloaded minds.

Unfortunately, brand and marketing folks can never agree on a definition for a brand, but most will come back to words like promise, expectations, preference, delivery, guiding idea, symbols and signals. My personal favourite is one I picked up from Bill McDonald, a mentor of mine: 'A brand is a promise that, when kept, creates preference'. At their core, brands work by setting expectations of performance against a set of needs that the buyer has and packaging this up in an easy-to-remember form. Once formed, we then take on trust that those promises will be delivered. Brands are a form of trust.

If trust as a form of social capital is well accepted, there is much more reticence about calling *brands* social capital. Reticence from the academic world because, perhaps, it cheapens the concept of social capital and from the business world for fear that yet another somewhat fuzzy, but also complex, concept is attributed to brands and branding. I will explore this tension later in this book because I think it is *essential* that we start to see brands as a source of social capital. I think this for two reasons:

- it recognises that brands and their marketing have a powerful effect on our society, effects that are permanent and, in some cases, change the way that we think
- because placing brands within a broader social framework means those organisations and teams that build brands are confronted with a greater responsibility for the impact of their actions on society and our store of social capital.

Stepping up to these responsibilities could seem like a threat, but I believe they are perhaps the biggest opportunity for business and brand-building ever.

Why they buy

'On-boarding', as the company calls it, is very well done at Procter & Gamble – it's not for nothing that this giant has earned its reputation for graduate training. As part of this training you are introduced to 'the consumer' – someone who is going to have a very great influence on your career as, at P&G, 'the consumer is boss'.

In the mid-1990s' a new discipline was evolving called consumer psychology. Departments and professors were popping up in American universities and consultancies were selling new techniques and frameworks. Of course, as you would expect, P&G was at the forefront of many of these efforts to understand consumers more deeply – this had always been the beating heart of the company even from its earliest days. So, everyone from the 'Class of 1996' was given a book called *Why They Buy? American consumers inside and out* (Settle and Alreck, 1986).

I have come back to this book recently and its central premise is that, by understanding what consumers want and giving it to them, a business can grow and succeed. Many companies are well advanced in their ability to do this – P&G, Coca-Cola, GE, Apple, succeed by fulfilling this premise by the promises they make. Other businesses, such as banks, are only coming to terms with this idea now and struggling with it.

Even as some succeed and others struggle, however, I believe this central premise is changing and needs to change. The relevant question now – given the challenges that we are facing in a hypercompetitive, globalised world, with the threats overconsumption pose to our environment, our communities and us as individuals – is, 'Why should anyone buy from you?'

Why *should* anyone buy from you?

Free markets and capitalism have worked. In the developed democracies, standards of living have never been higher. Consumption as a growth engine, ensuring demand outstrips supply – the core purpose of marketing – has been the greatest feat of human engineering in history. All this consumption has created a society, a world and even an image of us that, in many respects, is unrecognisable from what it was just 300 years ago. As is widely being recognised, the consumption trajectory we are on is unsustainable: there just aren't enough resources to go round billions more consuming as the West does today.

The challenges of sustainability that dominate much of the current debate in business come at an interesting time in the evolution of human communication. In the developed – and, increasingly, the developing – world the democratisation of communication through the internet is wreaking profound changes on the way that we gather, process and understand information about our world. We now have access to more easily accessible information than ever before. This is causing what has been called a revolution in transparency. There are fewer places to hide and, consequently, it is harder and harder to maintain brands that are not built on the mission and vision of the businesses that deliver them. Customers are more and more demanding and sophisticated in judging what is spin from that which is tangible. They are asking deeper and more searching questions of the brands and businesses that want their money.

It has been said that we are just starting a 'great transition', from one type of world to another, as we battle and hopefully resolve the challenges that face us as a global community. As with any transition, there is a range of potential outcomes and paths that can be taken. The question 'Why *should* they buy from you?' creates new landscapes that recognise the impact businesses have as a route to wealth creation, both economic and social. This is incredibly exciting as we create trust through our brands and marketing that is not just built narrowly on product performance and price, but on a broader basis that competes on social outcomes as well as commercial, where we see fewer 'consumers' to sell to and more 'people' whom we can serve.

This question must not be only a corporate one but also an individual challenge to each of us working today. Having run a large marketing team and budget, I know the tunnel vision that is so easily adopted when the pressure mounts and the business demands growth. There will be aspects of our working lives about which we will not be proud. While at Capital One, I was responsible for sending millions of envelopes of junk mail, most of which will have ended up in landfill. If you work in a marketing team, especially if you lead one, you have a tremendous opportunity to release energy and satisfaction by considering how you create a business that is trusted and trustworthy.

Navigating this book

The basis for this book is that there is a set of profound changes, both short- and long-term ones, that we are experiencing and will significantly change business and the brands and marketing they employ. These changes are causing trust to be challenged as new questions are asked and the answers are far from clear. Understanding these new questions and starting to formulate answers as to where they will take us will be important for business and brands as they capture the hearts and minds of people and build the trust that is so important for businesses to succeed and help deliver economic prosperity.

In the first part of the book, I lay a foundation for understanding trust more deeply. This is based on months spent poring over academic research. I propose some quite simple frameworks for analysing and measuring trust that I hope are both insightful and practical. They form the basis for the exploration of how to build trust in the following chapters.

The main part of the book presents a series of insights around strategy, brands, marketing and communications that will help create businesses and their brands which can command higher levels of trust. These are important because I think that, as individual and community relationships change, brands have the potential to support the available store of social capital and this is a good thing for business and society. I recognise that others may not share this view. These insights are based on my research and thinking, combined with emergent best practice and interviews with brand and marketing practitioners and thought leaders in trust.

Each chapter shares some insight, often some data and stories along the way, and discusses some ideas for building trust. Through the Action boxes – one at the end of chapter – I've tried to make the concepts practical. Where appropriate and illuminating, I've also included vignettes of the interviews that were completed as research for this book. Much of what this book discusses is strategically challenging, built from emergent trends and requires vision. What I hope is that the process of thinking about trust and strategies to create it will lead you on a journey where you can draw some conclusions for your own business and brand.

I close the book with a more forward-looking description of what I believe can be the twenty-first-century mission for business – the (re)humanisation of business. Many, if not most corporations, especially if they are listed, have focused far too much on the short term at the expense of long-term sustainable advantage. In this pursuit, they have adopted a mono-dimensional approach that places numbers, often only financial, as the operating system of their company. Some of our greatest economists and business leaders are now questioning this, including notable names such as economist Professor Tim Jackson, Jack Welch, ex-CEO of GE, and Sir Stephen Green, ex-CEO and chairman of HSBC.

Creating a more balanced approach that looks after the interests of both the shareholder and all stakeholders, in the past, present and future, will, I hope, be a fundamentally more balanced, sustainable and, ultimately, more trustworthy approach for business going forward. I think marketing has a huge amount to contribute to this change, given that its skill is in understanding and capturing value from human needs and wants. Brand-builders have an enviable set of tools and thinking to achieve this outcome and can be a powerful ally as business embarks on this journey towards balance. This is what excites me about the potential future role for business, brand-building and marketers.

There is no doubt that many of the themes in this book are idealistic and, in some cases, aspirational. I hope that I have combined this with more practical thinking about how the ideas can be put into action, but I make no apology for the vision outlined here. There are hundreds of books published on the 'how to' of marketing and many more about the practical issues and challenges that brands and marketers face, but what we need more of in business are people who challenge the strategic status quo and, through this, demonstrate their passion and leadership, not just for the customer but also for the role that business can play in society on a sustainable basis. I hope this book speaks, in some small way, to those change agents.

One of the causes of the worst recession since the Great Depression was business becoming mono-dimensional, valuing only the numbers and often on a frighteningly short-term basis. This needs to change, for the good of our businesses, customers and world. It's our intent, as businesses, that forms the basis for commanding peoples' trust. What I hope is that this book can contribute to the emergent view that sustainable business – and, therefore, brand success over the long term – is best achieved through this rebalancing of what we in business prioritise and value. I believe achieving this balance can be the mission of marketing and marketers and, with it, give a new leadership vision for the profession that will command a following which can help you rise to the top and fulfil your potential and your team's, your customers', your business' and your brand's.

Why trust matters

Without trust, living life would be impossible. Trust is the glue that binds us together with each other. Brands are part of a vital store of social capital – mess with that and we are storing up real trouble.

'Thanks be to God,' was the reply from the small congregation as the midday mass ended. Agnes, a regular member of the church, chatted with friends as they slowly walked out. It was a warm day in May as she began her walk home. She made slow progress, befitting her 80 years of age, carefully treading the pavements with which she was so familiar.

She turned the corner on to Darkes Lane at around 12.50 and could see the reassuring sight of the railway bridge ahead that signalled she was nearly home. Five minutes later, as she went under that bridge, Agnes Quinlivan was hit by half a ton of falling masonry that violently exploded from the bridge. The road was in chaos, cars destroyed by the debris strewn over a wide area. Agnes lay there unconscious as the sheer terror of the incident emerged from the clouds of ash and dust and noise.

Up above, on the tracks, there was a deathly creaking of tortured metal, steel and glass. The carriage lay on its side, broken and destroyed by the violence of the incident. Six passengers were dead or dying as the town started to respond to the disaster.

The scene was chaos that day in Potters Bar. Residents still remember the incident with pain as they tell their stories of heroism and tragedy. Agnes was comforted by a local hairdresser as she lay covered in rubble on that cold, hard street. She died later in hospital from her head injuries.

At 12.55 on 10 May 2002, on the tracks just outside Potters Bar station, the four-coach train 365526, travelling at nearly 100 miles an hour, derailed, causing the final carriage to jump on to the adjacent line and then flip through the air. On its way, it struck a parapet on the railway bridge and then slid hundreds of metres, eventually mounting the platform. In all, 7 people died and 70 were injured on that sunny May afternoon.

The investigation into the disaster eventually led to Network Rail, the owners of the track, and Jarvis, the private contractor responsible for its maintenance, accepting full liability for 'all legally justified claims brought by the bereaved and injured.' In November 2010, criminal proceedings were initiated against these two companies following an inquiry that clearly demonstrated a catalogue of failures leading up to the tragedy. Negligence and incompetence were clear, including an engineer choosing not to replace a nut on the points but, rather, use a chisel to try to improvise a repair. As late as the day before the crash, an engineering worker had reported 'lethal vibrations' in the area but, due to incompetent systems, the team that went to check was sent to the wrong end of the platform. The incident sparked a debate about the use of private contractors in the UK that eventually led to Network Rail taking maintenance back in-house.

The 10 May 2002 marked a turning point for British rail travel and was the culmination of two decades of change. As the media pointed out the next day, the UK railway system was fundamentally and criminally broken. As day broke the very next day, however, millions boarded their trains, just like the passengers of the 12.45 from King's Cross to King's Lynn had done, with lethal consequences, the day before.

A deeper understanding of trust

after a disaster ... despite all our fears ... we just carry on as normal

After a disaster, a strange thing happens: despite all our fears that there are serious, potentially life-threatening problems, we just carry on as normal. We *still* travel on trains, planes and automobiles without even a second thought for our safety.

Why is this? Could it be that we just filter out all information that doesn't fit our preconceived ideas? After the Potters Bar rail disaster, people got back on trains the very next day, while reading the headlines in every newspaper about how the UK train network was flawed and faulty to the point of corporate manslaughter. After the 9/11 attacks, we still flew, yet the media was telling us that 'terror' was round every corner. After the banking crisis, we didn't withdraw our money and put it under the mattress.

Perhaps we revert to type because we are good at judging risk and we know that the chance of being on a train or plane that crashes is, in reality, very low. There is much convincing research, however, that our ability to judge risk, especially when fear is involved, is not terribly reliable. That's why we are generally more scared of flying than driving, despite all the evidence showing that getting into a car is one of the most dangerous transport decisions you can make.

The answer is connected with our nuanced and sophisticated ability to judge trust. We have evolved to be very good at holding conflicting thoughts in our heads. Our trust in the railway at a rational, functional level is rather unshakeable, built up over years of experience. This can co-exist quite easily with a complete lack of faith in the companies running the railway. We can keep this more *emotional* mistrust and balance it against the more powerful *rational* trust that allows us, even with trembling foot, to step into that railway carriage. Trust is a many and varied thing, not easily decoded or defined – and that is where we shall start.

Easy to feel but hard to define

I've asked many people to describe trust. In most cases their faces relax and lighten, a slight smile appearing, as they recall the trust that is most important in their lives. A harder question, which foxes most people, is to define trust. Generally, their definitions don't really live up to their own rich experiences. For most of us, trust is easy to feel but hard to define.

Trust is almost the first thing we feel. As we leave the womb and are placed on our mother's breast, an instant bond of what is **trust is almost the first thing we feel** called ontological trust is created between mother and child that helps nourish the child both physically and mentally. As we grow, we develop trust in ourselves that manifests as self-confidence or self-doubt. There is the trust between people within a relationship that creates a bond of deep love or, as the psychologists might call it, emotional interdependence. Trust can flow between communities and groups, binding them together. These feelings and experiences, when aggregated, create a generalised form of trust that can bind whole societies and cultures together.

The psychologists and sociologists have provided a deep analysis of trust in its many forms using their own often impenetrable language of macro-social trust and micro-social trust, from primary to reflective trust. Despite the huge focus in recent years on who and why we trust or, more pertinently, distrust, much of this work has not been fully exploited by businesses, their leaders and their brands. There are six types of trust that I'd like to define (see Figure 1.1 and Box 1.1).

Figure 1.1 Six different types of trust

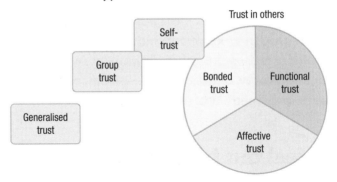

Box 1.1 Six types of trust

● **Functional trust** is the most basic form of trust and is focused on the delivery of a functional benefit. Functional trust is formed based on our early experiences of how the world works. It is enduring, more rational than emotional and difficult to change. Functional trust allows us to manage many of the basic aspects of life on auto-pilot – for example, trusting the sun will rise in the morning or the train will get me to my destination safely. Functional trust gets reinforced multiple times a day through many small experiences. When challenged, functional trust tends to bounce back strongly and quickly. High levels of functional trust explain why we keep riding trains after a rail crash or keep our money in banks even when they have been shown to fail.

- **Affective trust** is the next level of trust and is focused on the quality of our relationships. Akin to affection, it is based on how much we like and value the relationship. It is more consciously processed than functional trust and is therefore fragile. Affective trust takes longer to build and is more quickly damaged. Whereas banks, or at least the banking system, have high levels of *functional* trust, they have very low levels of *affective* trust – we use banks but we don't like them.

- **Bonded trust** is the highest level of trust and is usually reserved for the most significant relationships in our lives, such as with our children or life partners. It is more resilient than affective trust, but, if damaged, can have significant and lasting repercussions. Brands shouldn't aim to create bonded trust – it's earned and then bestowed, not demanded.

- **Generalised trust** is the general level of trust in a community, society or culture. It is characterised by loose affiliations. Organisations, such as community groups, churches and clubs, or even concepts, such as 'the American dream' or the British class system, form the backbone of generalised trust. Economies that can create the social capital of generalised trust experience higher levels of stability and growth.

- **Self-trust** is trust in one's own ability. All trust ultimately flows from a person's ability to self-trust. Without a healthy sense of trust in oneself, it becomes harder to trust others. Self-trust is built in the early stages of development and underlies the healthy giving and receiving of trust.

- **Group trust** When groups get together, especially within a framework that guides their behaviour, such as a set of values or a moral code, then group trust is created. Organisations that can foster high levels of group trust through a strong culture become more effective and reduce barriers to communication.

The nice guy finishes first

Game theory proves that the right strategy for success over time is to be 'nice.' This might be surprising, given it doesn't much sound like the way economists speak, but experiments have proven that the best outcome in a trust game is achieved by being the nice guy. These conclusions most often spring from the analysis of trust games such as the now famous prisoner's dilemma, where two supposed criminals are arrested and then separated and given a choice: stay silent or betray. Neither knows what the other is doing. If both stay silent, they each get six months in prison. If both betray, then they each get five years. If one talks and the other doesn't, then the blabber walks free and the other gets ten years. Normally, this situation is played out once and, 60 per cent of the time, participants choose to betray – preferring not to be stabbed in the back. The other 40 per cent choose to cooperate and take their chances, staying silent.

the right strategy for success over time is to be 'nice'

There has been much debate about what is the best strategy when the game is 'iterated', which is sciencespeak for repeated over and over again. Is it better to play nice and get to a comfortable, trusting relationship or take the dividend of the occasional betrayal or any other such variation? This was the question that Robert Axelrod, a professor of political science and author of *The Evolution of Co-operation* (1984), sought to answer when he organised a prisoner's dilemma tournament. He invited the cleverest of the world's experts in psychology and social science to enter a strategy that could 'win' an iterated prisoner's dilemma game.

The winner was a Russian mathematical psychologist called Anatol Rapoport. He entered the simplest set of rules: stay silent on the first move (be nice), trust the other guy and see what the other guy does, then, on your next go, do what he did (retaliate if he is nasty). Every so often, if he betrays, you can try to respond with silence and this forgiveness helps to improve the effectiveness. The conclusion was that the rational economic approach to the prisoner's dilemma – which is a strategy of betrayal that attempts to maximise individual chances – is less effective than trusting your partner in crime to help you. It's better to trust than not. You'll spend time in jail, but not that long and at least you'll have a friend!

A trusts B to do X

A trusts B to do X is the classic trust equation. A is the trust-giver and B the trust-taker. X is what is delivered and is important because this creates a level of risk that A is taking and creates expectations on the delivery of B. There must be some risk otherwise trust would not be needed.

Whenever there is a decision to trust, this is, either consciously or unconsciously, based on a complex set of interrelated signals and experiences that come together to guide the decision. This is especially true in the case of brands and creates a set of paradoxes. A brand trying to get consumers to buy uses marketing to provide signals to help the buyer judge trustworthiness. Advertising and marketing in all their many forms ask the consumer to give their trust by stating, at some level, 'I am worthy of your trust'.

These paradoxes that exist in creating trust cause angst for us. Trust is both rational and emotional, based on information and the lack of it, often reliant on competence or motivations unknown, is essential to daily life but also risky. What marketing and brands do is manage us through these paradoxes so that we feel we are making *good* decisions. When advertising works, it's on an emotional and a rational level, with marketing giving us enough information to draw conclusions about competence and, then, finally, the customer experience delivers against expectations.

The messages that flow from first exposure to the brand through to our initial interactions through to customer loyalty – need to balance the promises of a desired function, through to a level of affective trust that is built on a respectful relationship between the customer and the business.

Are people who trust dumb?

Increasingly, it seems that, in our cynical world, to trust is seen as perhaps foolish and to distrust smart. Toshio Yamagishi (2001), from Hokkaido University in Japan, created a series of experiments to examine the question 'Are people who trust dumb?'

Yamagishi asked thousands of students a series of questions about trust, including the classic test for generalised trust: 'Can most people be trusted?' Contrary to popular belief, he found that those who trusted more were better educated and more intelligent than those who showed less trusting behaviour.

He took the experiments a stage further by presenting a situation where each student had to judge the trustworthiness of a person when given different pieces of positive or negative information. These pieces of information were contextual, such as the person being judged had 'picked up rubbish on the street and put it in a bin' or 'pushed into a queue'.

What he discovered was surprising. He found that high trusters responded more sensitively to both the positive and the negative information. They were more attuned to making judgements about trust. The low trusters responded less positively to the positive news, but also less negatively to the negative news – their ability to differentiate and change their view based on new information was less well developed. Far from being a dumb thing to do, it turns out that to trust is a skill honed by the highly intelligent. Making finely balanced human judgements based on feeling and

far from being a dumb thing to do, it turns out that to trust is a skill honed by the highly intelligent

emotion, including about who, why and when to trust, are life skills essential to the successful human being.

When we expose ourselves to risk by deciding to trust, we get better and better at evaluating what signals to listen to and what to discard in making our decisions. If we shut this process down by *never* deciding to trust, as with the low-trusting students, then this important learning mechanism is not fulfilled (see Figure 1.2).

Trusting is an important part of being socially intelligent and, while it is an innate *tendency*, it is not an innate *skill*. Trust needs to be practised, with risks being taken and new information and experiences gained in order to hone our trust senses. Conversely, a vicious cycle of distrust and lack of social intelligence means that those who don't trust have their ability ever more blunted.

a vicious cycle of distrust and lack of social intelligence means that those who don't trust have their ability ever more blunted

Figure 1.2 If you don't trust, you don't learn

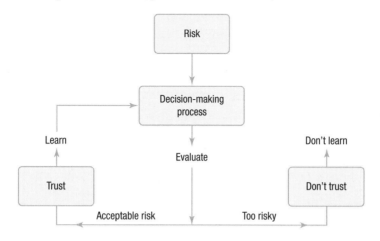

Free market free fall

In 1901, the hot stocks in America were the railways. They were growing fast and one of the largest was the Northern Pacific Railroad. This mammoth engineering project spanned the Great Lakes in the East to the Pacific in the West. There was a collection of companies that were developing and running the railways, with many investors large and small grabbing a piece of the action. Many fortunes, in reality and on paper, were made through this wild speculation. Illustrious names like J. P. Morgan, E. H. Harriman and James J. Hill were deeply involved.

As ever, these players were constantly attempting to gain an upper hand over each other and, on 17 May 1901, their fight spilt over on to the New York stock exchange. Harriman was making a play to take over the railways and Morgan and Hill were fighting. The stock market got wind that some of the Northern Pacific Railroad companies were going down and people were at risk of losing their fortunes, they couldn't trust the markets any more and they needed to 'sell, sell, sell'. As trust eroded, stocks plunged, trading was heavy and panic ensued – up to $75,000,000 was lost in the value of stocks in one afternoon with many small investors ruined. The beginning of a new century was welcomed by the now familiar pattern of trust destruction that leads to a stock market crash.

Throughout the decades, the same pattern emerges. The Wall Street crash of 1929 brought a calamitous end to an era of incredible speculation when over-leverage caused a widespread panic. In 1973, geopolitical trust was lost as OPEC declared an oil embargo in response to the USA supplying arms to the Israelis. In 1999, we lost trust in the Internet. Perhaps most striking, though, is the crash we are living through today. With the complexity of world markets and distributed risk, despite a seemingly robust regulatory and legal framework, when the system could no longer trust that subprime home owners in America could pay, the markets crumbled.

when trust is removed ... markets free fall

The painful conclusion that we keep unlearning is that, when trust is removed, whether in a company, a concept, shareholders or the actions of other countries, markets free fall. Suddenly the behaviour and outcomes that we have all depended on are no longer predictable and, therefore, can't be trusted. People and their decisions make the markets and people need trust. It's not money or the markets that make the world go round, but trust.

So what builds trust?

So, from our earliest developments as a human species, through to our advanced free market economy, being able to signal and build trust gives us an advantage. What, though, makes our minds up as we decide to trust?

The formula for trust is, at one level, simple: promise and deliver. This simplicity, however, belies a complex game of signalling and messaging exerting powerful influence over the instinct and attitude to trust.

The following elements build and support trust between parties.

- **Engagement and credibility** Trust requires engagement to begin with. There needs to be the opportunity to demonstrate trust and signal trustworthiness through an interaction, however small. From something as simple as asking for directions to asking someone to marry you, there needs to be a transfer of something, be that information, money, time or love. This context demands appropriate credibility. The man on the side of the road who looks like he is a 'local' has some credibility by want of his location and appearance. The nervous young man kneeling at the top of the Empire State Building with a diamond ring in hand hopefully earned the credibility he needs through his desire, his love and, of course, his purchase.

- **Setting and understanding the right expectations** Every exchange of trust is built on expectations – either implied or explicitly set. The expectation of food bought at the side of the street is different from that of food served in a restaurant. Expectations differ according to the specific experiences of the trust-giver. A person remarrying after a divorce is likely to bring a very different set of expectations into the decision to trust than someone marrying for the first time. The explicit or implicit motivation for entering the relationship is also a powerful source of expectations.

- **Honesty and respectfulness** Trust is built by demonstrating honesty and respect; mistrust is created by lying and being disrespectful. The truth is an important characteristic of any trusting relationship. This truth doesn't need to be agreement or a constant stream of good news, as long as disagreements or bad news are handled respectfully. The fact that marketing is often the practice of telling half-truths doesn't help build trust in brands.

- **Keeping commitments and consistency** The keeping of commitments is, as it were, the proof of the honesty and respectfulness pudding. There is nothing that destroys trust faster than not keeping commitments. The important thing, however, is to understand what promises are really being made in the mind of the trust-giver.

- **Trusting and being trustworthy** Finally, trust is a self-fulfilling and reciprocal process. The more you trust and are trustworthy, the more you will hone your instincts and the more you will build trust. The more trust flows between parties, the more trust is created. Many businesses fall down here – they just don't realise that trust is a two-way relationship and if they want people to trust them, then they need to trust back.

Appeal to the heart and the head will follow

Motivations are the current on which much trust flows. Charities, for example, are seen to be dedicated to others and the common good. It is this altruism that buys them an advantage in building trust. Businesses have largely lost the trust and understanding of people. No longer is it taken as a given that a profitable business, giving a good service and operating within the law is de facto trustworthy. The traditional arguments – that the profit motive leading to employment, tax revenue and economic success – are no longer enough justification for trust. This logic has crumbled due to a long history of bad communication that leads to businesses, and especially their leaders, being seen as self-serving. Increasing inequality dramatises this into a battle between the 'haves' and the 'have nots' and leaves people at a particularly low ebb in their trust of business and commerce. Enron, Equitable Life, fat cats and bankers' bonuses don't help business' cause.

People are more and more cynical and suspicious about the motivations behind businesses and their brands. This is where powerful leaders can come in as a clarifying, more trustworthy representation of the intent of the business. Richard Branson and the Virgin Group, Steve Jobs and Apple, even Jack Welch at GE in his day – all represented a vision for their brands and companies that help people get a clearer sense of where the company is coming from. These leaders are driven by a range of motivations that are greater than their desire to just make money and, thus, are perceived as more trustworthy. I attended Darden Business School at the University of Virginia a few years ago, where the irrepressible Jack and Carol Weber are fond of saying, 'Appeal to the heart and the head will follow.' In building trust, connecting heart-felt motivations with the actions of the business can be a powerful ally (see Box 1.2).

connecting heart-felt motivations with the actions of the business can be a powerful ally

---

Box 1.2 Humble in the face of your customer
An interview with Nigel Gilbert, CMO of VirginMedia and former CMO of the Lloyds Banking Group

'In a large number of institutions, especially the banking business, the covenant between the business and the customer has been stretched, often to breaking point. Banks, for example, have always tended to believe that their primary stakeholder is the

---

shareholder. They have, because of this assumption, decided that delivering the highest possible return is the most important thing.'

As we drank tea together in an upstairs room in London, I listened to Nigel discuss passionately the challenges and opportunities for creating trust in brands and businesses. Leading the development of not one but two major financial services' brand positionings – HSBC's 'The world's local bank,' and Lloyds' 'For the journey' – uniquely qualifies Nigel's insight into how brands, especially financial services brands, work.

'All institutions, but especially financial services, ignore a lack of trust at their peril. One of the positive outcomes that I hope for from the recent difficult period is a diminishment of the arrogance that businesses have often treated their customers and clients with in the past. Arrogance is a deeply untrustworthy and unattractive trait. You should always be humble in the face of your customer. They have a choice and you shouldn't simply assume their loyalty.'

'But how do you reorient these massive organisations towards the customer?' I asked.

Nigel paused for a moment and replied in his characteristically quiet and considered manner: 'They must look into their own hearts and really look at what they are doing. There is often a dichotomy between what companies *say* they are about and what they actually *do* – their actions and their words are different. Organisations need to be much more forensic about their activities, the impact of their actions and how they are perceived. They then need to adopt the right metrics, a satisfaction or recommendation mindset, to start to change their internal culture and processes. They then need to create a compelling idea, a point of view, of why what they do matters to different stakeholders.'

'How are organisations responding to these challenges?' I probed.

'These changes are difficult but the brand leaders of the future will be those that demonstrate active respect for their customer.'

I left the session with mixed feelings: positive that brand leaders like Nigel clearly had thought deeply about these important issues, but concerned that, just as our banks and financial services institutions seemed to need this thinking more than ever, leaders like Nigel were exiting the industry far too frequently.

Brands are stores of trust

It is now a cliché how many decisions and marketing messages we are faced with every day (thousands), but it is certainly true that, in our information-rich world, we are overloaded and brands are a useful shorthand for the qualities we are looking to find.

In the past, brands played the role of a 'guarantee' of product quality when a food or drink, for example, could kill you. Nowadays, given almost universally high product quality and strong regulation to guarantee it, brands act as a convenient and memorable idea, summarising a range of qualities and experiences that have been provided and promised over the years.

This storing of trust in a memorable, trustworthy idea is the economic purpose of brands. A brand is a short cut to the assumption of a positive set of qualities and, therefore, significantly reduces the transaction costs between buyer and seller. Without brands,

a brand is a short cut to the assumption of a positive set of qualities

buyers would have to do a lot more conscious processing and sellers would have to provide a huge amount more information and reassurance to gain a sale. Both these changes would increase tangible and intangible costs. Brands also have other interesting properties, such as transferability between minds, engagement and an ability to command loyalty. They are psychological entities hence they are inherently fragile and difficult to create consistently.

The experience of a consumer from first awareness through to product experience is most effective when it demonstrates the five trust-building elements. Marketing helps to present the brand idea, associate credibility and set the right expectations to build a basis for trust. The product or service delivery – the customer experience – then delivers honesty, respectfulness and keeps commitments. Organisational values and culture, together with their processes, are what ultimately deliver trust, not logos, marketing promises and advertising. The whole business needs to be aligned against the goal of delivering a trusted, trusting and profitable relationship.

The best brands and the organisations behind them are consistent. This is the most important aspect in creating a powerful brand. Through consistency, the right expectations can be set with credibility and this can be followed up by delivery. Mark Ritson, an associate professor of marketing at Melbourne Business School and award-winning columnist for *Marketing Week* in the UK, is fond of holding up Ryanair – the Irish budget airline, with its controversial CEO, Michael O'Leary – as a great brand. Ryanair, with its aggressive pricing and advertising, its choice of out-of-town airports and its CEO who claims that you will have to pay to go to the loo on a flight soon, is setting and delivering on a consistent proposition: the lowest-priced, most budget airline there is. For Ryanair, nothing gets in its way in the promising and delivering of the cheapest flights. It has a high level of functional trust and a low level of affective trust – and it is a highly effective brand. Nowhere does this say you need to be liked to be trusted.

The tools of the brand and marketing strategist – insights, benefits, reasons to believe, consumer segmentation, positioning, proposition development, advertising and media – are all focused on establishing that powerful engaged relationship with the right consumer. Trust doesn't have to be a differentiator, but it has a role in every brand, whether it is as a reassurance at the functional level or a relationship-builder at the affective level. Without it, brands have to try harder, which means spending more, to convince the consumer.

Social capital, trust and brands

Social capital and trust are really, really important to the well-being of our economy and our society. All successful societies and economies have built sophisticated approaches to enhancing and embedding social capital and trust. The rule of law, regulation, democracy, even the class system or the American dream, are ways of enforcing, either formally or informally, a behaviour system that helps ensure predictability and builds trust.

Businesses and their brands sit within this glue of social capital. There has, however, been a general reluctance for brands to be recognised as social capital for fear of cheapening the concept and, as Marek Kohn put it to me, 'the commodification of relationships' (see Box 1.3). Brands, though, are now an ingrained part of our culture and have incredible weight and resources pushing them. They are also part of the narrative of our communities and interactions. Communities form around them and opinions are sought and fought over. I think they should now be recognised as a part of our general store of social capital and trust. This, then, puts a deeper responsibility on business leaders and brand-builders to understand and care for their role in the creation of this social capital. This is both an opportunity and threat.

Box 1.3 Do brands and corporations build or destroy social capital?

An interview with Dr Marek Kohn, honorary fellow faculty of arts, University of Brighton, and author of Trust: Self-interest and the common good *(2008)*

Marek Kohn's extended essay on trust, published as *Trust: Self-interest and the common good* (2008), is a powerful set of thoughts

---

about how many key issues facing our society, from inequality to democracy, have at their heart the changing landscape of trust and how this important element of social capital is created or challenged.

As I sat waiting for the interview to start, I was excited since Dr Kohn was a distinctly different subject from the marketers, businesspeople and commentators with which I had been discussing the issue of trust. I was glad that he had agreed to speak to me. As we made our introductions, I mentioned the concept of brands as a source of social capital.

'Branding is certainly an important element in the commodification of relationships as corporate bodies and their brands replace relationships between people and communities. This means that relationships in this context are bought and sold. This makes it hard to argue that this process adds to the store of social capital', was Dr Kohn's opening salvo. I was certainly going to get views here that would contrast with the others I had gathered.

Dr Kohn continued, 'The use of brands as the public face of corporates and the reinvention of the individual with the constant affirmation of individualism in marketing has taken place at the expense of relationships among communities. And so the effect on social capital must be, surely, profoundly negative.'

What I was finding really refreshing in the conversation in these first ten minutes was the objectivity that Dr Kohn had on the world of business. Having thought deeply about trust he clearly saw business as just one, perhaps rather small or at least small-minded, realm; an element within the broader fabric of society and human relationships.

'To a certain extent, clearly the primary responsibility for a capitalist concern is to make a return for shareholders. This has certainly been the focus of the past few years and has, in many ways, led to the situation we are facing now.' Dr Kohn paused for a moment.

'So is business a "lost cause"?' I asked.

'No, far from it,' Dr Kohn replied, surprisingly emphatic. 'I can't see an overwhelming reason why this should be a one-way ratchet. Human societies have operated around communitarian or family or other forms of collectivism for hundreds of years. The rise of the individual is a relatively novel phenomenon, but, clearly, capitalism in its current form is too focused on the narrow.'

'How does business start to regain the trust that has been lost and become a greater net contributor to social capital then?' I asked.

'Well, I am persuaded that some people in particular businesses have a genuine moral vision over and above their focus on shareholders and, of course, there have been moral visions for business in the past, such as the great philanthropists and the model paternalistic employers. Clearly you *can* wield capital for purposes that are self-evidently more than just returning value to shareholders or yourself.'

Thick versus thin

The human ability for managing relationships is limited. Network theory has revealed that the optimum number of relationships we can meaningfully hold is somewhere around 150. There are many examples of how this has been a natural threshold. Armies, religious communities, villages, businesses – all have found that groups of around this number are most effective. Surely, though, with tools like Facebook or Twitter this number is now defunct? Well, the evidence would tell us, not really, with the vast majority of users of Facebook having somewhere between 100 and 200 connections.

If anything, what's changing is not our ability to hold 150 deep or thick relationships, but our ability to maintain many more thin relationships. 'Thin relationships' are, in many ways, at the heart of a society's store of social capital. Francis Fukuyama, in his masterful book *Trust* (1995), described how those societies with a greater ability to create generalised social trust through the spontaneous sociability of associations like churches or clubs create a higher level of social capital that can be drawn on in the creation of prosperity. The USA, Germany and Japan, for example, have rich traditions and processes that bind people together and, in doing so, mould and change behaviour, making it more predictable and, ultimately, more easily trusted. This has been fundamental to their economic success over the past century.

what's changing is … our ability to maintain many more thin relationships

What's happened over the past 20 years as our consumer society has grown is that brands have attained a deeper, thicker cultural context. We now feel comfortable sharing and interacting through and about brands. We talk, argue and desire brands. We use them to personify companies in a way that would have been bizarre to people even only 100 years ago. They form a narrative that changes our lives and relationships and moulds our behaviour.

The realisation that brands, the businesses that underlie them and the marketing that propels them into our collective and individual consciousness are a part of social capital is, for me, profound. This changes the rules and puts a greater level of responsibility on us. We shouldn't just adhere to a broad definition of the 'truth' in marketing but we must now also care about the individual and collective impact of our actions and messages on society as a whole. Getting our heads round this will be the only way to sustainably regain the trust in our brands, our businesses and our industry that we so badly crave. Trust is a complex and many layered thing. Brands are a big part of our trusting lives and recapturing trust in them is both a competitive and, when seen in the context of social capital, a societal problem.

brands … are a part of social capital

In this chapter, we've looked at the basics of trust and how this often nebulous concept works to create trusted businesses and brands. We are all living through a period of huge change in the landscape of who, what and why we trust. In Chapter 2, we examine how trust is changing.

TAKE ACTION TO SEE HOW TRUST WORKS FOR YOUR BRAND

Step 1: Gather evidence
- What measures are you tracking/insights do you have regarding the **functional** aspects of your brand?
- What measures are you tracking/insights do you have regarding the **affective** aspects of your brand?
- What do you know about your brands' ability regarding:
  - engagement and credibility
  - expectation settings
  - honesty and respectfulness
  - keeping commitments and consistency
  - trusting and trustworthiness
- Reach out to other teams (PR, investor relations, operations) to search for trust insights and data.

Step 2: What are you asking your customer to trust you for?
- Define what your trust equation looks like:
  - A trusts B to do X
- Who is A – are there different groups?
  - Do you understand their openness to trust and risk?
- Who is B – is this clearly defined?
- What are you really asking the customer to buy into? Examine risks and benefits.

Step 3: Where does trust in your brand come from?
- How well does your brand stack up against competitors regarding each of the levels of trust and the category average?
- Is the trust in your business mostly at a functional level (it works) or at an affective level (I like it)? Is bonded trust relevant to your brand?
- Build a framework for trust that puts your measures and insights against the different types of trust.

What's the matter with trust?

Is trust in free fall or bouncing back? Brands and the businesses behind them are seen today as serving the fat cats and their own selfish interests. Leaving it like that is the road to higher costs, more intervention and zero customer loyalty.

The view from the twentieth floor of the Westin Hotel in downtown Cincinnati would be, for many people, unremarkable but, every time I stayed there, I used to look down on the city, fascinated. The grid layout, the McDonalds and Starbucks, the yellow taxi cabs, the police sirens screaming past – all looked like they were from the set of a movie and were enthralling, but there was something missing.

On one visit, I was finishing a telephone call with my uncle in Milan, who I'd visited a few weeks before. I'd spent time marvelling at Italian life – the animation of the people, the noise, the colour and, of course, the girls passing by. The richness of the information about life that can be gleaned in an Italian town or city in early evening is amazing. Three or four generations walking together, the arguments between them, the news of the day being shared, how groups congregate and disperse – all tell the complex story of life being lived. I thought back to my high-rise view of Cincinnati and it dawned on me what was missing: there were no people. The Cincinnati streets were empty. The city wasn't dead – there was a very real sense that things were happening – just without people on the streets.

The decline and fall

Most Brits who spend time in America will bemoan how difficult it is to walk anywhere. Ask in the lobby of a US hotel if you can walk to a nearby attraction and you get some strange looks. In America, people drive and they do it mostly alone. Jane Jacobs, in her 1961 book *The Death and Life of Great American Cities* (1961), described the 'daily ballet' happening on the streets. The mass movement and information exchange between strangers going about their daily business. Steven Johnson in, *Emergence* (2002), extends this idea, identifying how, 'Sidewalks allow relatively high bandwidth communication between total strangers … [they] provide both the right kind and the right number of local interactions.'

Trust is declining and nowhere is this more acutely felt than on the street. It's always been the case that walking among strangers in an unfamiliar place has had a certain piquancy to it, which is, of course, half the fun of travelling, but these uneasy feelings are now more and more common as we make our way round our *own* communities and countries. We feel the impact of not knowing our neighbours, the fear of terrorist attack, the spectre of paedophilia and crime, as we move around with less comfort and more suspicion. What we are experiencing is the decline in the complex web of social capital that is trust in our surroundings and others.

trust is declining and nowhere is this more acutely felt than on the street

These rising fears create an environment of nervousness and suspicion that makes it harder for us to feel comfortable with others. We therefore naturally spend more time alone or in close family groups, in our cars and in our homes and less out in our communities. We turn more to television and the Internet for information and social stimulation and the narrowly defined groups with which we choose to associate. We lose our sense of ourselves as citizens, together with others in society, and often replace this with other roles, like ourselves as consumers. Marketing and many businesses benefit as we replace community with consumption. This vicious cycle is familiar to many of us who live in the big cities with millions of others, where we don't know 'the Jones's', even as we feel compelled to keep up with them. Depressingly, as our behaviour changes through this greater atomisation of our society, we destroy our very ability to trust, denying ourselves the opportunity to learn and interact with others, blunting our skill in trusting.

How is trust changing?

The evidence for changes in trust exists both in what we can feel and what we can measure. The measurement of trust is complex and often done poorly (see Box 2.1). Almost all credible surveys of trust show, time and time again, that it is diminishing around the world (see Figure 2.1). The landscape of trust globally is very different, however. Faster-growing economies – China and India, for example – tend to show higher levels of trust, as they see tangible improvements in their standards of living from the progress of their economies. The Nordic countries also tend to be outliers, achieving the highest level of trust, perhaps because of their homogeneity in social society. The USA and UK tend to generally occupy a middle ground, with the continental Europeans being the global sceptics.

Box 2.1 The tricky problem of measuring trust

- How much do you agree with the following: 'I trust brand X'.

- This is the classic market research question that is employed in brand-tracking studies the world over, but it is an inadequate measure, given the complexity of trust. Its inadequacy is demonstrated frequently by one survey saying brand or sector X is highly trusted and the very next month another saying the exact opposite.

- In many cases, trust should not be measured directly but inferred and modelled from easier-to -answer questions. People find it easier to answer a series of questions about *specific* attributes, such as honesty, respectfulness or keeping commitments or

---

consistency, than more abstract questions, such as 'Do you trust that brand?' Most often, the respondents, as they answer, are asking themselves the question, 'In what context?' If a direct question is used, then it should be defined as being directed to either functional or affective trust.

● Professor Christine Ennew of the University of Nottingham publishes every year the 'Financial Services Trust Index'. This splits out basic and affective trust into different dimensions for a more accurate read on trust. When, at the height of the financial crisis, all other surveys of trust were in free fall for banks, this survey was relatively static. That is because it accurately measures the high levels of *functional* trust in banking and the very low levels of *affective* trust. Clearly, as people queued up at Northern Rock, there was a blip in *functional* trust, but this recovered surprisingly quickly. Affective trust has continued at a low level because we have always hated banks and, until they change, always will.

Figure 2.1 Change in generalised trust over the past three decades

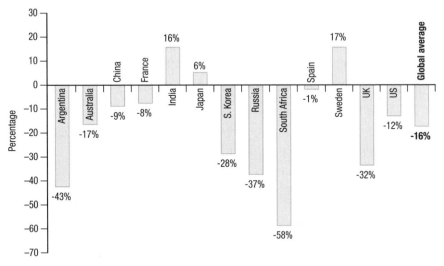

Source: Justin Basini, analysis of World Values Survey data 1980–2001

Who do we trust?

The traditional forms of authority that imbue trust are religious or hierarchical, such as the monarchy. Achievements, such as in academia, science, art or the professions, are routes to trust, but, as we change, what we class as achievements and who we place trust in is changing. For example, the achievement of gaining publicity is enough for many celebrities to command a high level of trust and credibility, even about subjects of which they can rationally have no detailed knowledge. Managers and politicians have no professional basis of achievement and, therefore, are less trusted (see Figure 2.2).

who we place trust in is changing

The picture of who we trust is relatively stable: doctors and teachers at the top and politicians and journalists at the bottom. Over the 16 years between 1993 and 2009, Ipsos MORI in its 'Trust in doctors: Annual survey of public trust in professions' (2009) measured a 22 per cent decrease in the trust held in business leaders and a 16 per cent decline in the trust ascribed to the ordinary man or woman in the street. The big winners – perhaps surprisingly – were government and journalists, although it should be noted that, even after prodigious increases in trust, only two people out of ten said they would trust them!

While these data are based on a limited definition of trust – who respondents say they 'trust to tell the truth' – it seems that motivations are the key to achieving high levels of trust. Generally 'altruistic' professions, such as doctors, nurses, teachers, are more trusted than 'commercial' or 'power-driven' professions, such as businesspeople or politicians. When those being trusted are *not* out for something for themselves, such as profit or power, then they are much easier to trust.

Figure 2.2 Who do we trust and how is it changing?

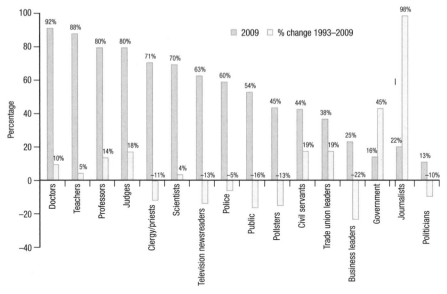

Source: Ipsos MORI (2009)

Note: Around 2000 British adults 15+ were asked the question, '… would you tell me whether you generally trust them to tell the truth or not?'

Do we trust business and businesspeople?

half the population or more claim they don't trust business (or government for that matter) to do the right thing

Trust in business is under pressure in the UK and Europe, with half the population or more claiming they don't trust business (or government for that matter) to do the right thing (see Figure 2.3 and Box 2.2). These data, from the '2010 Edelman trust barometer' (Edelman, 2010), again illustrate that trust is very different in different parts of the world, with the UK and continental Europeans at the bottom of the trust scale and the faster-growing economies, such as China, at the top.

Figure 2.3 How much do you trust business to do what is right?

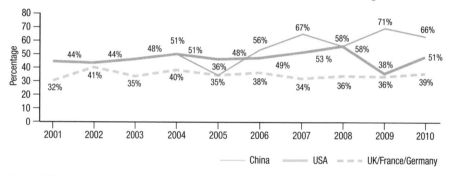

Source: Edelman (2010)

Note: Survey completed by more informed and educated people ('Informed publics') aged 35 to 64 in the USA, UK, France, Germany and China.

We can guess at the cause of this declining trust: the atomisation of our society, the increasing sense of individualism, the ending of the Cold War, financial collapses and recessions, cynical and fast-moving media, the decline in formal religion, global businesses failing – the reasons are multilayered and interrelated. After all the analysis is completed, however, one powerful conclusion can be drawn: our store of social capital, in the form of trust, which, historically, has been a powerful asset we have been able to draw on, is being, increasingly quickly, spent.

In brands we trust

'If you try to build trust just through marketing, you are on a hiding to nothing', said the CMO of a major brand when I interviewed him. 'If you need to *say* people should trust your business, then your business is most likely untrustworthy', he concluded.

The most trusted brands across the world are amazingly consistent. Pampers, Nokia and Toyota achieve most trusted status around the world, according to research by Millward Brown (see Table 2.1). Their metric of trust is called 'TrustR' and is a combination of 'How trustworthy is this brand?' and recommendation. By this measure, 48 per cent of brands had below-average trust, with 27 per cent achieving a 'good' score of 105 per

Table 2.1 The most trusted brands around the world – No. 1 TrustR brand by country

COUNTRY	BRAND
Australia	Colgate
Brazil	Porto Seguro
Canada	Toyota
China	Nokia
Czech Republic	Microsoft
France	Pampers
Germany	Pampers
Hungary	Nokia
India	Surf Excel
Italy	Nokia
Japan	Toyota
Korea	Cheju SamDaSoo
Mexico	Colgate
Netherlands	Douwe Egberts
Poland	Nokia
Russia	Nokia
Spain	Lindt
Sweden	Nokia
Taiwan	Nokia
Thailand	Nokia
UK	Pampers
USA	Amazon.com

Source: Millward Brown (2010)

cent of the average. According to its study, the No. 1 TrustR brand across 22 countries achieved a deeper bond with its customers, was 7 times more likely to be purchased and will steal market share.

Figure 2.4 The percentage of brands seen as trustworthy by the consumer has halved over the last ten years

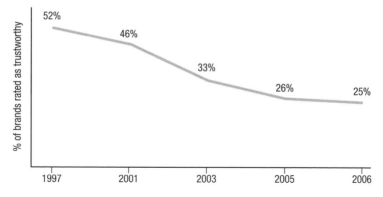

The landscape of trust in brands and business is not wholly positive, however. In their fascinating – and, in many ways, unsettling – analysis of brand value in *The Brand Bubble*, John Gerzema and Ed Lebar (2008) identify an increasing disparity between the value placed on brands on the balance sheet and the view of the consumer. The value of brands, according to their analysis, now account for 30 per cent of the value of the S&P 500, while brands are in decline on a range of consumer measures, including trust. Gerzema and Lebar present a triple threat that they believe is responsible for the increase in a sort of 'malaise' towards brands from consumers: excess capacity, lack of creativity and loss of trust. According to this way of measuring brands, the percentage of trustworthy brands halved over a ten-year period (see Figure 2.4).

the percentage of trustworthy brands halved over a ten-year period

Fear and greed

The reasons for the palpable change in trust are hotly debated and rightly so. In, *Trust*, Anthony Seldon (2010) describes ten reasons why the Western world especially is losing trust:

1 decline of religious and moral codes

2 decline of family and sense of belonging

3 continued social exclusion

4 corporate greed and corruption

5 rise of consumerism and the rights culture

6 the rise of violence and fear of violence

7 disappointment in politicians: scandals and expectations

8 the ubiquitous media

9 increase in accountability and surveillance by government

10 dehumanising scale and pace.

While it is clearly difficult to diagnose why trust is in decline, these forces are powerful in their scope and, I think, broadly right. I want to build on them and deep dive into the effects of business, brands and marketing, exploring what we can do, both as a contribution to the restoration of trust and for our own competitive advantage.

Despite the decline in trust, especially in relation to whom and what we trust, we still feel the powerful forces of trust and social capital moulding and changing our behaviour. Trust in each other and our peers have replaced much of the deference to authority that we used to rely on. As people in power have let us down, we have naturally turned to each other. Mistrust in institutions, businesses and the powerful, however, creates tension and increases transaction costs. Understanding how to reverse the trend and start to command people's trust again is important (see Box 2.2).

as people in power have let us down, we have naturally turned to each other

---

Box 2.2 Moving away from trust-destroying measures
An interview with Rory Sutherland, chairman of Ogilvy & Mather

Rory Sutherland is close to approaching legendary status in the world of advertising, especially in London. His stint as chair of the

---

Institute of Practitioners in Advertising heralded a new questioning of the role and approaches of marketing and advertising in business. He is an enthusiastic proponent of new frameworks for understanding how psychology and the disciplines of marketing interrelate to change society, people and businesses.

Just back from a summer holiday in France, Rory was in robust form as I started my interview with him. 'It's all very well to say that the shareholder is the most important group in a company, but that's not really true when employees might work for 20 years, customers may buy for 40 years and shareholders might hold on to the stock for a couple of days as a flipping exercise for short-term gain. Most businesses run through autistic measures,' he proclaimed, 'anything that is numerical triumphs over anything that is less measurable, less quantifiable and longer term, such as trust.'

He continued, 'You could argue that the shareholder value movement and the stranglehold of accountants over businesses have made them less trustworthy. Almost all businesses are obsessed with the short term and this makes it hard to build trust. There is a great phrase that trust grows at the speed of a coconut tree and falls at the speed of a coconut.' Having heard Rory speak several times, this was classic Sutherland – engaging, direct and challenging.

'So how can brands capture and build trust?' I asked.

'There is a huge amount of reciprocity in the building of trust and this makes it difficult for businesses. Much of the world's progress has been driven by commercial gain, but people tend to be vastly less grateful for your achievements when you are in it to make money. Human nature, to some extent, has an anti-business bias. When your motivation is greed, people tend not to trust', Rory explained.

I try to push towards a conclusion: 'So, surely, if that is the primary purpose of a commercial entity, there is no squaring that circle?'

'Well, brands and businesses that are founded and run by an

enthusiast rather than an accountant generally have more trust –
Virgin, Apple and Google for example. It's easier to trust these guys
because their primary motivation seems not to be money; they have
a passion for delivering their product. They and their companies
understand the emotional value that they generate and this allows
them to appear more trustworthy', concluded Rory.

'This is at the heart of marketing and advertising. Only a very small
part of advertising is what is said; the rest is in the nuance, the
presence and the emotional communications. We are programmed
to be much better psychologists than statisticians. What we have
evolved to do well is read all the social, unspoken signals and make
decisions to trust. What advertising does is say to the consumer that
the brand is taking an expensive risk to communicate and this says
so much more about the company than the advert.' Rory is on his
home ground now.

'It's so much easier for people to know the bad news of a company
more quickly than ever and this means that there are fewer and
fewer places to hide. I am hopeful, perhaps naively, that behavioural
economics, for example, can provide a way to bridge between the
more emotional behaviours of people and the more measurable
that businesses are so comfortable with. Perhaps this gives a
glimmer of hope, that, in the future, businesses can value both the
numerical and the emotional in their effects on the world.'

Doing a runner?

The next time you go out to dinner, I'd like you to consider something.
Try to position yourself near the exit and, when the bill comes, consider
how difficult it would be to 'do a runner' and leave without paying. I bet it
wouldn't be that hard. Next, consider not giving a tip. This is a somewhat
easier concept than not paying at all, but, if you're like me even this would
cause some discomfort.

It is likely that you have never even considered leaving a restaurant without paying. It's highly likely that you tip. The restaurateur and waiting staff trust us to do this. In most cases, there are very few control mechanisms to force adherence. So, why do more people not take advantage? It's because, while we are just grabbing a bite to eat, we are also conforming to a sophisticated set of social norms that build and help create social capital. Free market economics would have us believe that we all exist to maximise 'utility' or benefit to ourselves – that when we eat our meal, we deliberately calculate the cost and judge the value received versus our ability to get away with 'doing a runner' or not tipping. In reality, of course, and as long as the experience meets certain expectations, most of us wouldn't dream of not paying. Paying is a cultural, social and moral obligation.

Morality and the wealth of nations

Adam Smith (1776) implicitly understood this complex interaction between moral obligation, trust and the free market when he wrote *The Wealth of Nations*. Smith was a moral philosopher and spent his life dedicated to understanding ethics, rhetoric, jurisprudence, political economy and morals.

The ideas of morality, politics and economics sat much more comfortably together in Smith's time than they do now. In 1759 Smith published his first major work, *The Theory of Moral Sentiments*. He wrote about sympathy and social, as well as antisocial, passions; the effect of prosperity and adversity on behaviour and how merit and demerit can be used as rewards and punishment. He pondered how and why we act the way we do, how praise and blame change our views and behaviour.

morality, politics and economics sat much more comfortably together in Smith's time than they do now

Smith's framework was a discussion of morality and living a moral life. This morality led to greater predictability in behaviour and performance and this predictability could be trusted. These ideas were the foundational underpinnings of *The Wealth of Nations*.

The core concepts of *The Wealth of Nations* illuminate how important trust is to our economy. The 'invisible hand' is an elegant way to describe a set of behaviours and actions that form predictable market-based outcomes. Milton Friedman described it as 'cooperation without coercion' (Read, 1999: Introduction). Each participant must trust that the market will function within established norms.

Smith described how the division of labour increases productivity. Before specialisation, we would have grown wheat for ourselves. We would have harvested it, threshed it and ground it into flour. We would then have mixed it with other local ingredients and baked it into bread, by our own hands, taking responsibility for the whole process, from seed to food, relying solely on our own ingenuity and skill. In Smith's specialised world, however, we need to trust in the farmer, the miller, the baker, to produce a loaf that is safe and delicious. This specialisation is, in many respects, the conceptual foundation of brands.

Often the free markets that have arisen from Smith's theories are seen as cold and hard, prizing selfishness and individuality over everything else. This, though, denies the 'enlightened' nature of self-interest that Smith envisaged as being at the heart of his theory. This enlightened self-interest balanced the individual success and search for maximum economic utility with the common good and was tempered by a moral framework that ensured people acted for both themselves and the system. Smith understood that, in order to operate an efficient market, there needs to be predictable behaviours that create trust. He realised that, for an efficient transfer of value between buyer and seller, predictability was essential if trust was to be built. In other words, Smith knew that, in an advanced economy, the restaurateur trusts that we will pay and we conform.

Ethics versus morality in business

Seldon's identification of corporate greed, consumerism, fear and the media mentioned earlier all ask questions of business' current impact on society. Let's be clear, though, the social compact between enterprise, free markets and consumption has delivered an incredible amount to the Western world. Our standards of living, on average, are the highest that have ever been known in the whole of human history. These gains have been at the expense of equality, but, with the fast-rising so-called BRIC nations (Brazil, Russia, India and China), much more of the wealth is spreading around the world.

In the most capitalist economies, such as in the UK and the USA, however, something dangerous is happening. The positive outcomes from business are being replaced by malign ones. The hyper-competitive, short-term-focused, globalised, consumption-based system that we have created and benefited from is starting to compromise our well-being.

in the most capitalist economies ... the positive outcomes from business are being replaced by malign ones

The list of accusations is long:

- a cavalier attitude to the world's resources, step up the oil companies
- the globalisation of the supply chain to the detriment of the developing world and local production, step up the supermarkets
- the slavish following of consumer needs – sugar, for example – irrespective of the effects on health, step up the food and beverage companies
- the creation of passive, blind consumerism as a route to happiness, step up all marketers
- the blind faith in maths and the markets to make money, step up the banks

- fraud and dishonesty, step up Enron, Tyco and other corporate failures
- the intensive lobbying and power-broking to protect unsustainable industries, step up many commodity and manufacturing companies.

It's clearly simplistic to tar every company with the same brush, to write off business in general, but the result of all these issues is that the compact of trust between customer, consumer, the person in the street and business has been broken. This, despite the much greater emphasis, especially from business schools and big business, on considering business ethics.

the path that we were ... travelling along is unsustainable. People are waking up to this faster than business

Working in many businesses both large and small has become incredibly complex. It is no longer easy to see the impact of your individual actions on the world, the customer or even the business itself. You are a cog in an increasingly difficult to understand machine.

The past two decades of hyper-capitalism, resulting in the recent financial collapse and global recession, is a wake-up call. The path that we were, and probably still are, travelling along is unsustainable. People are waking up to this faster than business and its leadership. There is a need for change and those companies that can reorientate and recapture trust will be the winners. Marketing and brands as a route to social capital and as the visible beacons of their companies will play a significant role in this change.

Ethics need to be lived through actions in order to have any credence. I prefer the term 'morality' because it has a resonance lacking in 'ethics'. If something in a business is called 'immoral', I sit up and pay attention more than if it is called 'unethical'. The semantics matter little, but what does matter is how businesses can turn back to a clearer understanding and description of the morality of their actions and their impacts. This has to be the ultimate justification for why someone 'should' buy from you: because you do more good. That is something Adam Smith would have understood.

In this chapter, we've looked at the dynamics of how trust is changing in our society. People are concluding that business is untrustworthy and this is a major threat. How do the messages that businesses and brands put into the market as they seek to connect with people affect this landscape and either build or destroy trust? We will examine this in the next chapter.

TAKE ACTION TO SEE HOW TRUST IS CHANGING YOUR BRAND AND BUSINESS

Step 1: How is trust changing in your business?
- Examine the analysis you made when completing the action box at the end of Chapter 1.
- Do you know how trust is changing:
  - with your customer groups
  - within your category
  - with your brand
  - in the leadership of your business?
- How is decreasing social capital affecting your brand and business?
  - Are you being asked to justify more by the consumer?
  - Is regulation increasing?
  - Is social media exposing your brand to unwanted attention?

Step 2: Do you need to change how you measure?
- Are you collecting the right data?
- Does your data allow you to support your framework?
- Does your data match your gut feel?
- Do you need a trust index rather than just reading the score straight from a blunt trust question?

Step 3: How do you represent the role of your brand?
- How do you talk about the role of your brand in society?
- How honest are you about the value exchange that is going on?
- Do you make a fair return – that is, are the profits you make commensurate with the value you add to your customer and society and is it transparent?

Trust in marketing?

Are brands and marketing to blame for the mess we are in? Brands and the millions spent on messages to get people to consume have created the consumer society we live in. Adverts dressed up as independent evidence play on the destruction of our ability to think and resist. Our customers increasingly see through the half-truths and they often don't like what they see.

Helicopters and news crews descended on the mansion. Outside its impressive gates, photographers were pointing their lenses to try and get a peek at the life lived inside. The house and its owners clearly live the good life – manicured lawns and woodlands surrounded the many bedroomed house of pretty light grey brick.

As the couple inside paced in their kitchen, the tension was rising. Why were these news scavengers hounding them? They had done nothing wrong, nothing illegal. What right did people have to pry into their private lives? They had given over 30 years to public service and this was what they got in return. The anger and frustration at the seeming injustice of this invasion was boiling over. Action needed to be taken. He turned to the door and opened it.

Trudging across the driveway, several thoughts ran through his head. What will I say? How do I defend myself? Is this all worth it? The journalists descended and the pack started baying for answers.

He began his defence: 'I think I have behaved, if I may say so, impeccably and, what's more, I've done nothing criminal. And do you know what it is about? Jealousy – I've got a very, very large house – some people say it looks like Balmoral … As far as I am concerned, I, to this day, don't know what the fuss is about.'

The shouting and flashes from the photographers' cameras increased. He drew breath. 'This was a failure on my part. We have a wretched Government, which has mucked up the system and caused the resignation of me and many others. It was this Government which introduced the Freedom of Information Act and insisted on these things which have caught me on the wrong foot, which, if I had been cleverer, I wouldn't have done.'

'So you don't think any of the information should have been released', jumped in an eager young reporter. 'No,' came the reply. 'What right does the public have to interfere in my private life? None.'

That very afternoon, Anthony Steen's comments were on news broadcasts up and down the country, posted and pilloried on YouTube, the subject of hundreds of hours of analysis.

What was Anthony Steen's misdemeanour? Claiming £87,729 in expenses from the British taxpayer as a British Member of Parliament (MP), including payments for keeping his mansion and extensive grounds maintained.

From deference to reference

the British MPs' expenses scandal … will be seen as a watershed moment

The British MPs' expenses scandal has had, and will continue to have, a profound impact on the way that British democracy works. It is my belief that it will be seen as a watershed moment, symptomatic of a change in the way British society works.

The former British prime minister Tony Blair, in his political memoirs, *A Journey* (2010), has expressed a certain regret over the introduction in 2000 of the Freedom of Information Act. At the time, the Labour government hailed this as a powerful force for truth and transparency in society. They didn't foresee its ramifications. The Act has been used by citizens, including journalists, to get access to a wide range of information, from government expenditure and MPs' expenses to internal documents on a whole range of policy issues. These new freedoms to demand information combine with mass communications and the Internet to exponentially increase not just access but also the magnification of ideas and stories into the public consciousness.

The result is a profound shift in our assumptions of trust and our placing of faith. Whereas before people assumed a sort of blind faith or trust in people like MPs by wont of their position, this has now gone. Many have called this a move from an age of deference to the age of reference.

In the past, we would have chosen the path of least effort by deferring to those in positions of authority or power. Now, we often arm ourselves with information about their performance, their credentials and learn about the details of a particular issue. Doctors frequently bemoan the fact that patients come armed with information gleaned from the Internet on their range of real and imagined health problems. Something has changed.

Blink or think?

Malcolm Gladwell, in his book *Blink* (2005), glorifies our human ability to process many, many pieces of information, to divine a 'gut feel' almost instantly that is usually accurate and can be trusted. Over thousands of years of evolution, we have developed the ability to process a wide range of social signals that we are swimming in to guide our judgements. Often these are snap decisions about what and who to trust.

The trouble with these 'blink' decisions is that they can be easily manipulated. Manipulators deliberately employ psychological and social tricks to effect one outcome or another. Marketing is founded on these abilities and uses them to get us to change our behaviour and buy. Almost the first thing you are taught as a young marketer is the power of the 'single-minded benefit' and that this must be focused into advertising that has one idea running through it. There is little room for complexity or nuance. The well-crafted 30-second TV advert works to get us to buy because it employs emotional and rational cues behind a single idea and drives it home through repetition. Marketing teaches us to accept the surface and not dig any further.

This, in turn, has been both exploited and further compounded by the increasing pace and demand for news. The 30- or 60-second segment on the news channels is now the regular feature. Complicated and often difficult issues are reduced down to the most gratuitous aspects of the story. What gets magnified in this approach is often that which appeals to our baser instincts, hard-wired into our blink responses. Disengage higher-order brain and engage what Seth Godin (2010) calls the 'lizard brain.' No wonder, then, that our modern world is seemingly mired in things like sex, murder, corruption and threat around every corner.

Gladwell's *Blink* provoked a response from Michael R. LeGault, a former columnist from *The Washington Times*. In his book, *Think: Why crucial decisions can't be made in the blink of an eye* (2006), the central premise is that a wide range of forces are combining to degrade our ability to apply critical thinking and reason to problems and this is leading to poorer outcomes. He blames marketing partially for this race to the bottom, for its part in helping to create a culture where we blindly accept our role as consumers and give in to the marketing messages, taking them at face value. Critical thinking becomes the preserve of the few. This results in a 'loss of the ability of reason to influence people, policy, and institutions that is leading to a decline of good outcomes in America and Western civilization as a whole. It is *the* central challenge of our time to change this mindset.'

> **a wide range of forces are combining to degrade our ability to apply critical thinking and reason to problems**

From deference to preference

It's my belief that, because of this compromise in our ability to think critically, we have moved from an age of deference to *preference,* rather than reference. The choices we make today are mostly based on a blinking gut feel about what we prefer. We are given a set of simple stimuli that operate on many psychological levels to help us choose what we prefer.

Take the great myth of choice. Most research says that, contrary to the widely held view in marketing that more is better, choice is stressful and difficult; that's why default options are so powerful. What choice does is move our attention away from the fundamental questions, such as, 'Should I buy this', to surface questions about what colour or features or brand do I prefer.

If we *had* truly seen a change from deference to reference, wouldn't we see much more deep inquiry, more analysis, more thinking about the choices we make? No, what we have today is a world where we are sated by what we prefer. Even the analysis that does get done moves our attention away from true interrogation. For example, in the UK, all schools publish the results of standardised tests taken at the ages of 9, 11 and 14. These are pored over by the press and parents alike. While useful as an *extra* piece of evidence, these results are now the *main* focus when parents are choosing which school to send their child to. The responsibility of the parent to think critically about the type of *child* they have and what type of *education* they want for that child, in an attempt to find a suitable school based on both qualitative and quantitative inputs, is replaced by a rating or percentage achievement rate.

The age of preference is not just led by marketing. Changing educational focus, consumerism, declining standards in public life, an aggressive and unrelenting media and the sheer enormity of many of today's problems all cause people to switch off and turn to simple answers. It is these simple answers that brands tend to provide.

Marketing exploits the process of critical thinking. The classical presentation of an insight, benefit and reason-to-believe uses shallowness presented as evidence to get people to prefer one choice over another. This is its power. Good advertising works on an

good advertising works on an emotional and rational level, not to shout and bluster, but persuade us to prefer

emotional and rational level, not to shout and bluster, but persuade us to prefer. We are left with a world where spin and presentation in the drive for preference is what wins out. For businesses and their brands, this means that we build the basis for trust not on the true performance, quality or drives of our businesses, but on the surface power of our marketing and brands to spin.

Often this isn't the marketers' fault. 'We are the best house on a bad street' is a metaphor used to justify why our product or service, with all its faults, is still the best choice. Businesses are often unwilling to take the increase in costs or wait the time it will take to really create a good product that can honestly sell its virtues. Other options are rarely explored. What if the right thing to do was *not* sell a substandard product or highlight other areas of pride over and above the product, such as company culture, contribution to community or sustainability? (See Box 3.1)

Box 3.1 'Trust is created over years, not via a 30-second ad'
An interview with Mike Hughes, director-general of ISBA – The Voice of British Advertisers

You might expect the guy whose job it is to be the defender of the advertisers to be one of the black shirt brigade – not a Mussolini supporter but, rather, one of those Charlotte Street advertising and media types. Actually, Mike Hughes is an extremely down-to-earth marketer and general manager who holds distinctly practical views on the role of marketing and advertising.

'People have become more savvy about advertising, and ways of avoiding it if they don't want it, but advertising clearly does have an important role to play in helping those people form connections with brands that are increasingly expected to show leadership beyond their functional delivery.'

Leadership is a theme that Mike comes back to again and again. 'Smart marketers are realising that brands need to have a social philosophy.' This is especially important as government takes a

---

step back from seeking to direct peoples' lives. Businesses, via their brands, need to recognise their role as major 'change agents' in the way that society develops.

'The business and brand leaders that I talk to in my role accept the need to be sensitive to a broader set of needs across their different stakeholders. This is an important component of winning and retaining the trust that is vital to create great brands. The conversation at the top of business is changing.'

I butt in, perhaps a little too forcefully, 'But the data shows that people don't trust advertising and it's getting worse.'

'The fact is that politicians and parts of the media are over-fond of laying the blame for deep-seated social issues at the door of "advertising", which is not helpful. Consumers are not dumb; they know that advertising is about presenting a brand in its best light – they will then decide, based on brand delivery (or not), whether the brand merits their continued trust. Dove, Ariel, Lloyds TSB, HSBC – all these brands know that achieving and retaining trust is about delivery and consistency above everything else. Advertising, while important, can only provide the stimulus – after that, its down to the consumer.'

The conversation flows and we move towards the increasing sophistication of marketing and advertising to change our minds and influence our behaviour. 'What responsibilities do we have?,' I ask.

'Businesses and brands have clear responsibilities, in two senses. Firstly, to consumers, where the responsibility is to not mislead, and the UK's proven system of self-regulation takes care of that aspect very well. However, brands also have a real sense of responsibility *to themselves* not to blow the trust established over time, via either inappropriate advertising, or, more importantly, non delivery. Trust is created over years, not via a 30-second ad', concludes Mike.

Programmed to want

We are programmed, through messages, to want the new. From our iPhones to our ideals, we have largely replaced our role as citizen with the role of consumer. Jon Alexander, a young radical and founding contributor to Conservation-Economy (www.conservation-economy.org) who turned away from being an ad man, puts it like this:

we have largely replaced our role as citizen with the role of consumer

Consumerism takes the act of consumption and turns it into the defining act of our role as social beings, rather than one expression of that role. We all consume, but in a healthy society, we should also participate to an equally significant extent in social groups and relationships that are beyond consumption. We should produce, and we should be citizens. But in a Consumerist society, these other roles fade into the background. And this is dangerous, because with our roles as producers and as citizens (among others, perhaps) go balance and perspective in our societies. As Consumers, we become the centre of the universe. We have an inflated sense of our own importance. We have no real responsibility to anyone other than ourselves – we must look after our own interests first and foremost.

These points are most poignantly underlined by the response of the then President George Bush and Prime Minister Tony Blair to the 9/11 attacks, when they told us that all we needed to do in response to the disaster, in effect, was go shopping, though Bush maintains he did not use that exact phrase.

Convenient truths

Brands and the trillions spent over the years on marketing to propel them into people's minds have operated on some convenient truths that make our lives as marketers and the impact of our work easier to bear.

The first is that all advertising does is enable choice and doesn't make us buy more stuff. Common sense and our day-to-day experiences surely challenge this myth. The weight of advertising today is truly astounding and people constantly complain of overload. Globally, hundreds of billions of dollars are spent trying to flog us stuff. To claim that this doesn't have an effect on overall consumption is absurd.

The second myth is that advertising doesn't work on a subliminal level – all we do is present cogent arguments and evidence to aid people's rational decision making. *All* advertising and marketing works on a subliminal level – full stop. To be clear, I don't believe that this is a consequence of any Machiavellian plots by the 'mad men' (and women) of advertising, but a consequence of which we are fully aware, of the way that human beings process information. We judge adverts, brands and products on an emotional and a rational level and good advertising appeals to the heart and the mind. The science of persuasion has become so sophisticated that it works on many levels to effect changes in our behaviour. Sociology, psychology and now neuroscience have been exploited by marketing to effect the outcome marketing wants, which is for people to consume.

sociology, psychology and now neuroscience have been exploited by marketing to effect the outcome we want, which is for people to consume

In isolation, a single marketing campaign probably doesn't make much of a difference to our impetus to consume or change what we think or feel, but to deny the effect, in aggregate, of hundreds of billions of dollars spent on these messages is nonsensical, and, I believe, irresponsible. Marketing and its tools, in conjunction with the mass media, have created the consumer society.

There is a powerful symbiosis between mass marketing and mass media that surrounds each of us with messages programming us to consume. We are told that if we have newer, sexier, better stuff, we will be happier and more is always better. Although there are many underlying themes to this matrix of messages, one of the constants is fear and one of the consequences of this is increasing hysteria, unhappiness and mistrust. Unlikely as it may be, Marilyn Manson described it well in the Michael Moore film *Bowling for Columbine* (2002): 'keep everyone afraid, and they'll consume.'

Responding to media is trained into us from the earliest of ages. I opened the door of my living-room recently to be confronted by my four-year-old son, Daniel, 'praying' to the television. He was watching a programme on children's BBC called *Yoga Babies*. The fawn-coloured, massive-headed character on the screen was demonstrating a cross-legged exercise where you move your head towards the floor. Daniel was following and, in so doing, gave the impression that he was worshipping the TV. Even though he wasn't, this was a powerful metaphor for me about just how powerful the television is in so many lives and from the youngest ages. According to Dr Aric Sigman in *Remotely Controlled* (2005), more than half of all three-year-olds in America have a TV in their rooms, rising to two-thirds by six, with the average hours watched daily as high as five. From ADHD to our changing values, television has had a significant effect on all our lives and marketing paid for it.

The values that marketing and advertising portray have changed the way we think and feel about ourselves, our lives and what is important. As marketers, we play with and change what is trusted and distrusted in our attempts to try and persuade consumers to buy from us.

people, with greater access to information than ever before, are starting to see behind the messages and, often, they don't like what they see

The trouble is that people, with greater access to information than ever before, are starting to see behind the messages and, often, they don't like what they see. They are becoming more empowered, more demanding and raising the bar. People are increasingly concluding that they can't trust businesses and their brands, their advertising and their motivations. Despite the thousands of good people working for businesses, we are less trusting and more cynical of them. This will either result in increasing costs as we have to try ever harder to persuade, reduced prices as everything commoditises or zero loyalty as consumers assume that all businesses and brands are as bad as each other. This is a scenario that we would do well to avoid.

The challenge now facing our brands, our businesses and ourselves is how to move towards a more sustainable, better model where we can feel better about what we do, commit our brands to building positive social capital and regain the trust of people. We start to look at this in the next chapter.

TAKE ACTION TO SEE HOW TRUST IS CHANGING YOUR BRAND AND BUSINESS

Step 1: Ask yourself the hard questions
- How does the consumption of your brand help:
  - customers
  - shareholders
  - the environment
  - employees
  - society?
- If you stopped selling your brand tomorrow, who would benefit?
- If you stopped selling your brand tomorrow, who would be harmed?

Step 2: Become a conscious marketer
- What assessments do you use to assess your role's impact on the world?
  - How do you stack up?
- How much does your brand increase or decrease the store of trust and social capital in society?
  - Does your brand use fear or greed to sell? Is this right?
  - Is your brand virtuous in its actions?
- What is your macro-marketing scorecard?

- What is the effect on people when they experience your marketing?
- What effects would your marketing have if it was the only thing that people saw?
- How does what you do reflect the positive contributions of your company?

Beginning the journey to trust

Trying to command trust *just through marketing and you're on a hiding to nothing. Businesses that win trust get on a mission, understand deeply the relationship they have with their customers, communicate signals of trustworthiness and behave in ways that deliver the brand ideal.*

There was tension everywhere in the air. The yellow stench of gunpowder hung thick on board. Men all around were worried, their minds flitting between the task ahead of them and wondering if they would ever experience their life back home again.

Life in the British Navy in the early nineteenth century was unremittingly hard. Boys as young as eight were put to work with men, many of whom had been press-ganged or forced into servitude on the ships. Many were dressed in little more than rags and food was basic at best. Disease and distress were commonplace. Every waking hour was spent wishing for a life away from the boat and achieving this before your time ran out – average life expectancy was less than 20.

Discipline could be brutal and inventive. Perhaps you might be asked to spend your time after an offence shredding and then the retying rope so that knots and hooks were embedded in the ends. You'd then be flogged with it until your back ran red.

Among the tar blackness, though, was a glimmer of something that was worth fighting for, worth dying for. Horatio Nelson. This was a man who had fought and won, who bore his victories hard – blind in one eye and missing an arm – yet he wasn't that different from you. A gentle Norfolk boy, he'd worked his way up from the age of 12 to the exalted ranks of the British Navy. His patriotism and dedication to his beloved country was unwavering, his motivations clear.

This was a man who commanded, even demanded, your trust, bravery and devotion. Every man, whether a captain or cabin boy, who sailed to Trafalgar to meet a French fleet that outnumbered and outgunned them, felt safe in the knowledge that they were being led by the most capable and trusted British hero ever known.

Commanding trust

Nelson didn't command trust by accident or by his position; he worked at it

Nelson didn't command trust by accident or by his position; he worked at it. His many victories, often against unpromising odds, were as much a testament to his management style and strategic thinking as his bravery.

Nelson was a child of the Royal Navy, on board a boat from the age of 12. He had lived and breathed the life of the ordinary men and boys on board. Many of the innovations in his management – 'the Nelson touch,' as it has been called – have lasted right until today. Against a culture of strict adherence to hierarchy, Nelson was a natural communicator who placed emphasis on developing battle plans with his captains jointly. They were well understood and simple to encourage captains on their own boats to seize the initiative in battle. Nelson had never been reprimanded for brave but dubious decisions that he had made in his career – he wanted to encourage risk taking.

Unheard of and frowned upon, Nelson used to breakfast with the midshipman on his boat to understand his views and seek his feedback. He knew that the behaviour of his men in the heat of battle and their commitment to him and the cause was what would make the difference. He used to go below deck and visit men at their stations to check how they did things and do what we would call today on-the-job 'coaching'. It is said that, even as he was taken down after being fatally wounded at the battle of Trafalgar, he paused to give some advice to a sailor on the tiller.

His most precious strength, though – something that coursed through his body – was his unwavering commitment to his country. His motivations and desire to win could not be doubted. His intent was clear, his actions unstinting and his words inspiring. The trust that his men had in him was what made the difference.

The last order he gave at Trafalgar – 'England expects every man to do his duty' – took his beloved Navy into the most glorious victory in all of British maritime history. Even a few hours later, as he lay dying, his final words were famed to be, 'My God and my country'.

The sizeable prize of trust

brands exist in people's minds. They are essentially a collection of ideas and associations

Trust is a precious and complex entity. Brands exist in people's minds. They are essentially a collection of ideas and associations that, in totality, either make sense and can be trusted or don't and aren't. Forming these associations is far from easy, yet, as we've seen, brands like Toyota, Nokia, Colgate and Pampers manage to consistently out-perform on the dimension of trust. What is it that these brand leaders do to so powerfully to sway people's trust.

As Nelson knew it is a difficult problem to systematically command trust, but the prize is great. There are some consistent themes that could hint at the elements which contribute to creating trust. The first thing to realise is that the aim is not to *create trust* but create an *environment* where trust can be nurtured and promises delivered.

Trust can't be a window-dressing exercise. Some insights will work to effect trust in the short term at just a communications level, but, without the hard work of creating a business that can systematically build trust with customers, you are on a hiding to nothing. Businesses and their brands need to restore trust and re-establish the argument about their purpose and role in our society through honest hard work and straight talking. Unless they do, we will see increasing transaction costs and a continued decline of generalised trust and associated social capital across the developed world. This will not be good for our economies or communities.

Towards a framework for building trust

There are four things that are important for harnessing trust. This is what the best and most trusted businesses do (see Figure 4.1).

- **On a mission** What is it the business actually wants to achieve?
  - They are on a mission that is virtuous and helps achieve a sustainable balance of positive outcomes between stakeholders.
  - They compete on social dimensions as well as commercial ones.
  - Their marketing teams and leaders 'represent humanity' and create value across all stakeholders, not just customers.
- **Understand** They understand deeply the role and balance of benefits and risks within the relationship and transaction.
  - They deeply understand the role of trust within the category.
  - They deeply understand the role of trust for the people to which they are selling.
  - They balance and recognise risk as well as benefit in their promises.
- **Communicate** They signal trustworthiness by using their communications to set the right expectations on which they can deliver.
  - They deeply understand what promises are being made.
  - They recognise that the communication process is not a single point in time.
  - They match their signals and messages with their brand reality and aspirations.
  - Engage in the conversation to co-create the promise.

● **Behave** Once the right signals have been communicated, these need to drive customers and employees to the right behaviours in order to deliver the promise. The best organisations are high-trust cultures. They create a culture of trust and signal it both within and outside the organisation.

- They trust their customers and show it.
- They are true to themselves and play their own game.
- They see transparency as an enabler, not a shackle.

This framework, like all attempts to structure a set of thoughts, is not a panacea or one size fits all approach to fixing trust for brands. I hope that it will make us think and, in the following chapters, allow us to deep dive into issues that are important to structuring a solution to your particular business issue. In the rest of this chapter, I will outline the key background to each step in the framework.

Seek to understand

Throughout all my interviews and investigations in preparation for writing this book, time and time again, I was struck by how the best brands and their

Figure 4.1 Get on a mission, create compelling communication and drive behaviours

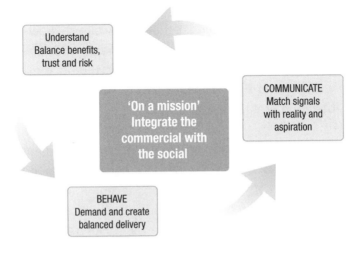

the best brands and their leaders intuitively and deeply understand the bond of trust that they are building with their customer

leaders intuitively and deeply understand the bond of trust that they are building with their customer. Cathryn Sleight, the ex-marketing director of Coca-Cola in the UK, told me about her experiences of building trust models at Coke. Mark Ritson told me about how Virgin, through their laser focus on positioning the brand and capturing an attitude, deliver an experience that commands trust.

Trust is not equal in all categories or businesses. The different levels of trust all work differently in different types of products. In transport, for example, functional trust is pre-eminent, whereas in computing, affective trust is much more important. In some categories and markets, trust is a differentiator; in others, it is a table stake. As we've learned, trust is also very context-dependent. The purchase of a Phillippe Patek watch for £15,000, on the basis it is something that will 'last for generations', is a very different trust decision from the purchase of a Swatch for £40.

Understanding the market and consumer context is important. As we deal with the fallout from the financial collapse, repay our individual and national debts and deal with the environmental consequences of an economy built on mass consumption fear will continue to be the dominant trend of the next decades. As we've moved from greed to fear, the recognition and understanding of the risk as well as benefit represents a significant opportunity for brands to differentiate and form stronger, more real connections with customers. Understanding the risk that a customer is taking and then helping them deal with these realities can create deeper more profitable relationships.

Understanding risk is something we are not good at. For example, Lucian Camp, the chairman of advertising group Tangible and an independent consultant, looked at the communications of financial products in the 1990s' recession in the UK and compared them with those in the most recent recession. Many of the brands in the 1990s' recession used the harsh realities of unemployment and economic uncertainty to connect with potential customers. Fast-forward to the recession of the last few years and financial advertising has continued to be dominated by 'people dancing down the beach.' Focusing overly on the positive means that the reality of life is largely denied in marketing. Most marketers today have only practised their trade in good times, so find it difficult to connect through risk and downbeat messages. They will need to learn.

the reality of life is largely denied in marketing

Box 4.1 We are wired to trust
An interview with Robin Wight, Chairman of The Engine Group

Robin Wight is one of the most visible and memorable characters in the London advertising scene. With his penchant for purple suits and pink shirts he makes a colourful sight in The Engine Group's slick headquarters on Great Portland Street in London. Robin in my experience is a classic agent provocateur, taking a view to an extreme position for sport and then using the cut-and-thrust to form and reform the real opinion.

'We are wired to trust – it's a biological thing. Trust is not a luxury; it developed through evolution because it conferred an advantage to those that had it. Seeing trust as a key part of the persuasion make-up of people in this way means that commanding trust is not a choice but a pre-requisite. Trust helps us choose with less brain effort. We get status when we are trusted, it's fundamental to reputation, this creates a feedback loop that keeps things honest but we are becoming less and less tolerant,' says Robin emphatically.

'How so?' I asked.

'Failure becomes more and more visible, more and more quickly today. Yet paradoxically products are more and more reliable and better than in the past. We've become less tolerant and our standards are much, much, higher. We are spoilt, we expect everything to work all the time. Consumers satisfy not optimise. In a world where product quality is so high we choose the brands that choose to engage us. This changes the rules of the game of marketing and brand building fundamentally.'

We discuss these elements of the changing game: 'We have a much greater need for emotional engagement today. We've been through a period of a rational centric model but I see this polarising. I think we are going to see deeper, more satisfying, emotional, pleasure-focused experiences when you are committed to a brand; whereas when you are in the market for a new product the buying process will be much more rational using information and tools to assess value and propositions. You see this most clearly in the mobile phone market. The brands are all focused on developing emotional connections with their loyal customers and acquiring mostly on price.'

'So how do you create trust in a brand?' is the next question that I put to Robin.

'It's a complex myriad of things. We all trust continuity, the brain likes consistency. We like reliability. If you keep giving different answers to the same question, even over years, you will find it difficult to be trusted. This is a major issue with brand repositioning – what you change can signal inconsistency and that can result in trust being undermined. Clarity, openness, and delivery, all of these are important elements in the trust equation.'

'You need to manage expectations tightly, over-promising makes building trust much harder. Building low risk, inexpensive ways to signal that you trust your customer are also very powerful ways to tap into the reciprocity of trust. Trust is a two-way thing and many brands and businesses too often forget this.'

Communications that match signals with the brand reality and aspiration

People see brands and businesses developing much more slowly and through a slow drip of their attention rather than a waterfall. Marketing and marketers can often fall into the trap of just focusing on one campaign at a time, especially when the pressure is on to acquire new customers or drive volume.

Any new communication, therefore, must be seen within the context of previous and future promises. Extending your brand into a new category, for example, will signal many subtleties to the consumer about your ambition and your commitment to the relationship around the core product.

The best brands are in control of their narrative. To watch Steve Jobs delivering an Apple presentation about their latest product is to witness a brand in complete control of the development and evolution of their narrative. They build on previous messages, reinforcing key benefits, and bring to life the mission, motivations and culture of Apple through actual achievements. This cannot help but move the brand forward over time.

the best brands are in control of their narrative

Marketing is, by definition, how a brand *wants* to be seen rather than its current brand reality. This is a real headache and causes immense difficulty for businesses and their marketers. The best understand this and develop strategies to overcome it. For example, the offer of a money back guarantee, such as has been used by Oil of Olay, or free returns, in the case of Zappos, or developing a narrative about change, such as Virgin Trains – these messages provide positive reassurance and buy the brand the permission to fail on occasion and not damage trust.

marketing is ... how a brand *wants* to be seen rather than its current brand reality

Driving behaviours that command trust

Getting organisations to do anything consistently is like herding cats. A strong culture and set of principles helps to create an environment for consistent action, in turn creating the right environment for trust to grow both internally and externally. Much as people who have low trust in themselves find it harder to trust, organisations that don't have a trusting culture internally find it a challenge to win the customers' trust. Srini Gopalan, Consumer Director for Vodafone UK, talked to me about the power of creating an environment of high trust within the organisation: 'Creating the right examples from the top and then incentivising the same behaviour in the organisation can quickly create a culture of positive intent and trust.'

Creating that culture of trust enables a set of behaviours to emerge that can be powerful in delivering against the brand ideal. The fastest way to create a trusting relationship is to promise something relevant, manage expectations tightly and know that your organisation is going to deliver. Once customers have been won, though, many businesses choose to assume a position of distrust with them. They start to provide worse service, such as having *sales* call centres in the UK and *customer service* ones abroad; they extend worse offers to existing customers than to new ones. Loyalty and long-standing relationships between buyers and sellers are rarely factored into decision making. The bond of trust is broken because businesses quickly leave the impression that they don't trust the customer.

loyalty and long-standing relationships between buyers and sellers are rarely factored into decision making

Strong internal behaviours are built from a strong sense of purpose and principles. When I worked with him, David Nichols, now a partner at The BrandGym, used to rail against the anodyne nature of most mission statements and corporate values littered with the same old words: quality, innovation, value and customer focus. These are price of entry attributes today; what we really want to know is what makes you culturally different. This gives the business the confidence to be true to itself and play its own game – in turn, driving authentic and original action, creating predictable and repeatable actions in which the customer can trust.

When we observe a brand getting this dynamic right, then it is powerful. The rebirth of Marks & Spencer, the British retailer, under the leadership of Stuart Rose is a good example. The brand turned back to its history authentically, its people and its customers. While turning back, though, it also didn't shy away from taking responsibility for issues that it is contributing to now, such as environmental challenges. 'Plan A', as it is called, is an elegant attempt to put at the heart of the business a set of environmental policies that make a significant contribution to both the top and bottom lines of the company. These initiatives have helped M&S to re-establish itself as a brand leader, reconnect with its customers and also cut costs.

Get a mission

Most corporate mission statements are complete and utter rubbish, containing stereotypical, Dilbert-style, generic promises that mean little to anyone. They rarely represent what many businesses actually do or care about. For example, almost never do they mention making money and, if they do, they couch this in vague terms, like shareholder value. Most businesses are on a mission to make money in some way, shape or form. As rare as a diamond is the mission statement that actually says this and inspires beyond this.

as rare as a diamond is the mission statement that actually inspires

Evolution has taught us to look for great leadership because that way we were more likely to eat and less likely to be killed by a woolly mammoth. We are programmed to trust leaders who stand for something more than just making money. The 'something more' is what is appealing and, in our changing world, with so many problems, we want to connect, work with and buy from these people and their businesses (see Box 4.1).

Box 4.2 To thine self be true

An interview with Chris Satterthwaite, CEO of Chime Communications

'Being big makes it harder to be trusted because it becomes more about the business and its performance than the mission – profit should be a byproduct of the core delivery of the business. The very best brands create connections based on authentic experiences that sympathise with and understand the customer condition.'

I saw Chris Satterthwaite first talk about the issue of trust at a Chime Communications symposium-style event. At the time, brands were in the eye of the trust storm and this was a significant piece of leadership, pulling together brand owners with brand thinkers to discuss bespoke Chime research on the issue. What I liked was that the event forced the 100 or so attending to work with each other to really look deeply into the heart of the lack of trust in business and come up with ideas.

Now I was sitting opposite Chris in Chime's head office in Mayfair. We were really starting to get to the bottom of the problem, which was clearly one that Chris had thought about deeply over a career that started in brand management at Heinz and led to his rise to CEO of Chime Communications, a network of marketing communications businesses.

'Times of crisis breed the need for trust and leadership,' Chris said as he answered my question about how we build back the trust in brands. 'This leadership can come from brands as long as they are consistent to a core set of beliefs and values. Without this, a brand can become rootless and this is hard to trust. Ensuring that you stay true to thyself is the only way to convincingly ensure that what you say matches what you do.'

Chris continued in a determined, quietly spoken way: 'We are clearly in a dip in trust. How long that dip is no one knows. Decades ago, the best businesses were heroes creating wealth. They are now often seen as zeroes, but we are already building back to a period of neutrality. Those that continue to demonstrate their commitment to their own beliefs in delivering value to customers will be those that will move back to strength. The challenge for many is to pick what they keep and identify to change in order to regain people's trust.'

A business goes through many manifestations – different leadership, different markets, different customers. Yet, we all realise the trust value of consistency and reliability built and invested in over the long term. A period of success is often followed by challenges and, as businesses respond, there is a fine line to tread between understanding the true heart of the business and deciding what to remake in the journey to deliver consistently while always trying to remain relevant.

'Something more' is a concept that Tom Farrand, a collaborator of mine and founder of brand and innovation consultancy The Pipeline Project (see Box 9.1, Chapter 9), and I call the 'social imperative'. As we have discussed, the assumption that business is a de facto source of well-being has largely faded. The days of Rowntree, Wedgwood and Cadbury using business to improve the lives of workers and customers as a direct consequence of their creating profitable businesses are long gone. Bill Gates and Warren Buffet make their money in the commercial realm and then give it away. I admire this philanthropy, but I think we need to create a new vision for businesses where, through their core businesses and the making of money, they also deliver quite deliberately a social good. Grameen Bank, the micro-finance lender that started in Bangladesh, is a very pure and easy-to-understand example of where the more they do their core business, offering very small loans to poor people, the more good they do. They also make a profit.

We are more aware than ever of the impact of our actions on the world. These impacts are increasingly seen as a consequence not just of our direct behaviours but also the behaviours of those businesses and brands we favour. Buying a Coke or a Big Mac becomes a more difficult decision than it once was when it is mixed up with bigger issues, like the rise in obesity or water shortages or deforestation of the Amazon. Putting petrol in the car or turning on the heating become guilt-ridden as we become aware of their impact on the environment. Purchase decisions have become much, much more complex.

people are left with a strong sense of disappointment and disillusionment. The irony is, this presents the biggest opportunity ... that has ever been known

There is increasing unease that we as 'consumers' are being played and manipulated into a descending spiral of negative outcomes for ourselves, the communities we live in and our world by businesses. Whether this is a conscious strategy, conspiracy theory-style, or an unconscious result of actions without thought to the bigger picture is largely, I think, irrelevant. The overall result is that people are left with a strong sense of disappointment and disillusionment.

The irony is, this presents the biggest opportunity for brands and businesses that has ever been known. That businesses have a social impact is self-evident – this particular genie is out of the bottle when so many of the largest economic entities in the world are businesses. The businesses that realise they can compete for people's trust and loyalty not just by creating fantastic products and services but also in terms of the social impact of their activities, will engage on a much deeper level and command respect through their virtue. It is these businesses that will get on a mission, understand, communicate and behave in a way which will deliver a deeper connection to their customers' heads, hearts and wallets, using trust as a key competitive advantage.

In this chapter we have started to examine the overall elements of the journey back to trust for brands and businesses. There are higher goals to fight for that will enable brands and businesses to reconnect and be forces for good, inspiring people, whether they be employees or customers.

We next move on to look at the changing realities for consumers as they evaluate which brands they want to buy.

TAKE ACTION TO ESTABLISH YOUR OWN FRAMEWORK FOR TRUST

Step 1: What is your mission?
- What is your brand's mission?
- What is your corporate mission?
- What effect – commercial and social – do you want to have?

Step 2: What are you promising?
- What are the benefits you are promising?
  - Higher order?
  - Lower order?
- What are the risks you are solving?
- What fears are you exposing or dealing with?
- Are your promises honest and straightforward or do you over-claim?

Step 3: What are you communicating?
- What signals do you think your customer needs to give you trust?
- How do you currently signal your trustworthiness?
- How does your advertising help support your appeal for trust?
- How do your marketing plans help to build trust?
- Are your communications consistent over time?
- Are your communications integrated across silos?

Step 4: How are you behaving?
- How are you delivering against your promises?
- What is your brand reality?
- What is your brand ideal?
- What is your brand aspiration?
- How well do your internal missions/visions/values support your brand's promises?

The new realism

People are questioning more and more. No wonder this leads to a crisis in trust when marketers are over-promising and their businesses under-delivering. The 'new realism' is that there is a more fearful, more risk-aware consumer who wants to connect with brands that provide solutions to real problems.

I opened my notebook as I pushed the tape into the video player. An image fuzzed on to the screen; it was of a small bathroom. The picture was grainy and faded. Slowly, a Japanese woman walked into the bathroom. She proceeded to turn the water on and it started to fill the small but high bath. The water looked hot and steamy. Removing her clothes, she stepped into the water. Her knees were bent towards her chest as she sat, the depth of the bath allowing her to be almost completely immersed in the water. Her sense of relaxation could be seen as her muscles relaxed in the hot water. She took a moment to enjoy the sensation.

Picking up a white flannel, she poured a little gel on to the cloth and rubbed the cloth between her hands, creating a lather. With this foam, she washed her body slowly and meticulously, starting at her head and working down. She paid particular attention to certain areas, such as behind her ears, her armpits and elbows, using the flannel to scrub and clean. Washing her whole body took ten minutes and, when she had finished, she got out of the bath, satisfied.

Her body was dripping wet, but the small room was warm as she took a towel and dried herself in a deliberate fashion. The image on the screen froze and then cut to another bathroom. I waited a moment and another woman walked in and started to wash. I turned the page of my notebook as I watched.

I can't get no satisfaction

This story is not a confession of a fetish for watching women wash, although I am sure somewhere on the Internet there must be a site dedicated to this particular peccadillo, but, rather, a description of part of the job that I did at Procter & Gamble (P&G). This sort of product research is happening every day across the world in the search for things to satisfy the consumer and gain competitive advantage. What I was watching was a video of women's washing habits around the world, from Japan (extremely fastidious) to Germany (fastidious) to Britain (less fastidious). All the women were paid handsomely for being studied, were entirely consenting, were never fully naked and all ethical guidelines were followed, but, in hindsight, it was still a bit weird.

Procter & Gamble was the first company to systematise this type of research in a big way – they have referred to it as their 'stealth advantage.' A mythological story told to young recruits at P&G recounts how Tom Halberstadt, in the 1930s, took a train ride to Philadelphia to see why Lever's Swan bar soap was beating P&G's Ivory soap in product tests. He went to visit women in their homes and he asked one to wash the dishes in front of him. He discovered that she just threw the soap into the sink, added the water, placed the dishes in and then took each dish out, washing and cleaning it as she went. When he observed women doing this with the Lever product, there were plenty of suds, but, with Ivory, there were none – hence, the product failed to give a strong signal of its cleaning power and, therefore, lost in the tests. In the lab, the scientists were rubbing the plates with the soap to clean them, so they were optimising for the wrong thing.

Wolfgang C. Berndt, an executive vice president of Procter & Gamble, in a speech in 1997 to the American Marketing Association's Doctoral Symposium, said that the company is, 'at its innovative best when we can bring together what's truly needed with what's truly possible.' He recounted that, between the end of World War II and 1960, P&G launched over 15 major brands that are still household names today: Tide, Crest,

Head & Shoulders, Fairy and Pampers among them. These brands are some of the world's most trusted. All are founded on achieving P&G's mission of 'improving the lives of the world's consumers.' The techniques that are employed in the pursuit of this goal are increasingly sophisticated. In the same speech, Mr Berndt stated that one of the company's aims was to 'understand consumer needs on a profoundly different level than our competitors – and on a deeper level than our consumers.'

The system that P&G invented and has practised for generations breaks the process of developing and selling products down into a series of calculated steps. The product must be superior, meet a consumer need, fit the brand and have claimable advantage in advertising. The selling process should be focused on a 'single-minded' benefit that can be captured in a 30-second TV commercial and will resonate strongly with the consumer. The pricing should be premium and discounted only very rarely.

Each step is tested in a logical fashion using rigorous, standardised and comparable tests. The P&G system is widely admired and has been replicated around the world and across different industries.

This has delivered better standards of living, ease, convenience and time for the consumer and to P&G one of the best-performing stocks. The constant search for delivering consumer satisfaction – more recently, consumer 'delight' – has kept people consuming. Always searching for deeper ways to influence – some would say 'manipulate' – consumers to buy and stay loyal, there has been increasing movement away from the functional to 'higher-order' needs. Brands and products are no longer about cleaning your clothes, they are about caring for your family; nappies (diapers) are no longer about capturing faeces and urine but being a better mother; soap is not about cleaning, but revealing the best of yourself as a woman.

This constant search for higher-order benefits is what famed psychologist Abraham Maslow called 'self-actualisation'. Anyone working in marketing over the past few decades will be, most likely, intimately familiar with Maslow and his hierarchy of needs, which has become an accepted 'truth' in marketing and advertising.

The validity of this entire way of thinking about people and our needs, however, has been questioned. The hierarchical nature of the framework naturally pushes marketers to the higher order – who wants to just satisfy lower-order needs? Why are human needs a hierarchy, though? Manfred Max-Neef (1992), an economist and philosopher, has challenged the notion that we satisfy our needs sequentially, ticking off one level and then moving to the next. He believes that *all* needs must be satisfied for contentment. Others have criticised the hierarchy for conforming to a particularly Western view of what is important.

people are smarter than ever at decoding and seeing through the marketing promises and over-claims

I think, however, that the most powerful and biggest criticism of the hierarchy, especially the search for 'self-actualisation', is coming from the postmodern, tired and cynical consumer who has endured years of marketing messages. People are smarter than ever at decoding and seeing through the marketing promises and over-claims. They are recognising that soap or shampoo won't and can't turn you into a super-mum or supermodel.

Brands are starting to prove that exposing this paradigm and tapping into the debate about it is a powerful way to connect. A good example of this is the Dove (a Unilever brand) 'Campaign for real beauty'. This campaign has successfully engaged with and contributed to the debate about images of female beauty by using real women, diverse bodies and diverse faces to provoke and connect. It has moved the brand into unique and fundamentally more honest territory. The issue for this campaign – and why Dove eventually moved away from it – was that, while it was an amazingly brave and brilliant piece of communication, it was not mission-led, either from a Dove or Unilever perspective, and was therefore unsustainable.

The 'new realism' that is emerging is here to stay (see Box 5.1), as we battle debt, recession, slow growth and question the good of unfettered consumption. For the majority, the world is now about dealing with the hangover of the consumer boom. Those brands that continue to promise the Earth and deliver little will continue to exist in a shallow world where trust is difficult, to build.

Box 5.1 'Trust is a human, personal and fragile thing'
An interview with Cilla Snowball, Group Chairman and Group CEO, and Farah Ramzan Golant, Chairman, AMV BBDO, London

Cilla and Farah are a friendly but formidable force in the advertising industry, running, as they do, one of the most famous, successful and stable advertising businesses in London – Abbott Mead Vickers. Visiting their Marylebone headquarters is to witness a living, breathing advert for their work. Client brands and the advertising that is produced for them by the agency is everywhere, which is maybe why their 67 clients stay with them, often for decades and decades.

'There is a fine line between faith and trust. Every brand wants to be trusted, but building trust is painstaking. Trust is fragile and human.' This interview was revealing something more emotional and deeper about trust.

Cilla continued, 'Creating trust is part of the duty of care between a business and its customers. Brands are a two-way dialogue today – a trusted business must have a willingness to listen, to take feedback, to gain different perspectives, to show their values and what is important to them.'

Farah quickly jumped in, 'Building trust in a transparent world is all about having and sharing this point of view, articulating it well, building it from a strong set of values that explain how and why we do what we do. So many businesses either don't bother explaining or don't even truly understand why they do what they do.'

'What do we really mean by trust? Trust at a hygiene level guarantees performance, but leadership comes from a higher set of values that can create engagement and create human bonds, even love.'

'But is love really something a brand should aim for?' I asked.

After a few moments, Farah answered: 'Love is powerful but, for a brand, it is bestowed through the hard work of trusted delivery over time – it cannot be demanded. Truly trusted brands don't assert their point of view; they present a choice openly and create systems that ensure they will deliver. There is maths and magic in creating a trusted brand.'

Through their work with clients such as Sainsbury's and *The Economist*, AMV BBDO powerfully demonstrate the need for brands to create ideas that put these thoughts into action. Connecting with people should be at the heart of all good businesses, from advertising through to delivery. Outstanding brands understand the fragile nature of trust and the power of values.

You think in benefits, but your *customer* thinks in risks

A major consequence of this rapidly changing worldview is that the awareness of risk is much greater. Risk of losing your job, risk of damaging the planet, risk of the bank going bust – these are the realities of today's world for most consumers. Smart marketers will start to acknowledge this changing environment and readjust their processes of development, marketing and communication to take advantage. Without this readjustment, the current dislocation between the reality of peoples' lives and the sunny world of marketing will continue to contribute to the loss of customers' trust.

This dislocation is apparent in a lot of marketing today. It can be seen in the airbrushing of images of beauty or manipulation of advertising, such as the L'Oréal advert for a mascara that creates long, luscious lashes, yet the model is wearing lash extensions or the use of toys to attract young children and their parents in to McDonalds or the constant product churn to persuade us that the old but perfectly serviceable is worthless in the face of the new. As Dennis Bagley says in the film, *How to Get Ahead in Advertising* (1988):

> We're living in a shop. The world is one magnificent f**king shop, and if it hasn't got a price tag, it isn't worth having. The greatest freedom of all is the freedom of choice, and that's the difference between you and me, boil.

The world as a shop, where I can fulfil my every desire by buying more stuff, has, I think, run out of steam. People are questioning their actions and those of companies more deeply than ever. This is both a threat to business and a fantastic opportunity to reconnect through realism. This has the potential to build trust and social capital and help gain competitive advantage.

I asked Marek Kohn, an author and expert on trust, if we could change from passive consumerism to a world where we make more active choices. He replied, 'We've got ourselves into this mess but, only in the past 100 years or so – we survived perfectly well before, and we can turn back the tide creating something fundamentally better.'

people are questioning their actions and those of companies more deeply than ever. This is both a threat to business and a fantastic opportunity

Risks are much more important to people in their assessment of their choices today than previously. People are looking for much more balance. Global consumer research (Mintel, 2009) has shown that the current major global consumer trends are:

- the need for resilience in a changing and uncertain world
- consumers reviewing and reassessing their decisions and looking for greater balance
- ethical and environmental responsibility
- stability and security regarding jobs, crime and more global instabilities

- escapism
- empowerment through greater access to information.

This search for more balance is a response to the significant changes in the world landscape over the past decades.

- **The rise of cynicism, an accountability culture and loss of social capital**

  Creates questioning from individuals and society about whether or not consumption and using brands to gain a sense of self and achievement is right. The increasing disquiet that, as we define ourselves as consumers, we lose a sense of community linking us to each other and our society as citizens.

- **Increasing instability and changing geopolitics**

  The defeat of communism, the rise of individualism and unfettered free market capitalism leading us to collapse, has left a huge sense of instability and insecurity. This has combined with the War on Terror to create a much greater sense of personal threat and insecurity. People are assessing risks differently than

Figure 5.1 The move from higher-order needs back to lower-order risks

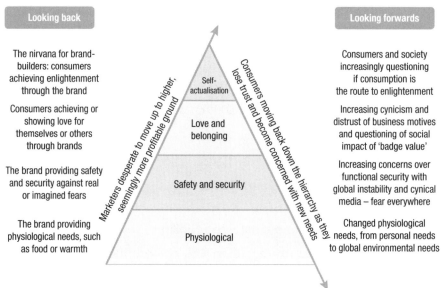

in the past. Aspects of their lives that would have received scant attention in the past – such as 'Should I fly?' or 'Is it safe to keep my money in a bank?' – are now being reconsidered.

● **Business, growth and consumption seen as malign**

Increasingly, business is seen not as a force for good but a way for the few to feather their own nests. This inequality leads people to distrust business and its leaders. There is also a growing sense that growth for growth's sake is not a recipe for happiness and well-being, either individually or collectively. This narrative is becoming more mainstream. People are increasingly questioning their consumption, for its effects on both the world and themselves.

● **Consumption in opposition to the environment**

Physiological safety and security need to reassert themselves again. The unprecedented environmental challenges the world faces and the sense that we are 'using up the world and its resources' far too quickly leaves people, once again, questioning safety. This is not immediate product safety, but the longer-term safety of the product in the world in terms of environmental damage.

This seeking of balance between new lower-order needs and new ways to attain higher-order needs (see Figure 5.1) is a major part of the understanding that needs to be developed of changing beliefs, allowing a fertile, real connection to be formed with consumers as the basis for trust.

Fear and risk

In their book *Nudge*, Richard Thaler and Cass R. Sunstein (2008) shared an experiment they developed that powerfully illustrates how we magnify loss.

They took a class of students and gave half of them coffee mugs with the insignia of their home university on them. Those who didn't receive a mug were asked to examine their neighbours' mugs. Those given the mugs were then asked to sell their new possession to those unlucky enough not to get one. All the students were asked the following: 'At each of the following prices, indicate whether you would be willing to give up your mug/or buy a mug'.

The results showed that those little mugs become twice as valuable to those who had been given them originally than those who would want to buy one. Giving up something you have hurts much more than acquiring something. Thaler and Sunstein concluded, 'People hate losses. Roughly speaking losing something makes you twice as miserable as gaining the same thing makes you happy.'

Loss and the fear that it invokes changes our behaviour and causes us to act irrationally. The above example of what Daniel Kahneman and Amos Tversky (1979) called 'prospect theory' is just one example of how our psychological biases affect and distort our behaviour. We respond to fear powerfully. We are much more frightened of falling out of the sky in a plane accident than crossing the road, even though the latter is much, much more dangerous.

Marketers and salespeople have known for a long time that fear and loss sell. Our knowledge is getting more and more sophisticated as psychology and economics come together and we can understand how human behaviour changes under certain circumstances. Fear is the 'lower-order' stick and the brand is the 'higher-order' carrot. Think about the antibacterial products that now crowd our shelves for a perfect example. They fight invisible, unquantifiable enemies – bacteria – that we have been told time and time again are dangerous. They fight it in

fear is the 'lower-order' stick and the brand is the 'higher-order' carrot

a way that we can never assess, but, if we don't buy this brand, we are, according to the ads, putting our children in grave danger and being irresponsible parents. We will get the cuddles and adoring looks of affection from our children when we make this brand choice. In reality, every parent knows that the kids will never notice and, if they are anything like my kids, will need to be cajoled and harangued to ever use the stuff.

While this one campaign idea might not have an effect on the overall level of fear in society, combined with the media and all the other fear-based messages out there from other brands, it does contribute to an overall negative impact. Fear, in this case, then, affects social capital by making people more worried, stressed and less trusting.

fear ... affects social capital by making people more worried, stressed and less trusting

This is not to deny that encouraging the washing of hands is not important – it has been called the greatest health intervention ever – but antibacterial soaps and cleansers are not massively more effective than ordinary soap and water in the fight against bacteria. They are, however, better for marketers in that they can dramatise the situation and command premium prices for the products, making ordinary soap seem somehow inadequate.

Human beings have a difficult relationship with fear and risk. Ulrich Beck (1992), a German sociologist and professor at the London School of Economics, coined the term the 'risk society'. He used it to sum up societies where risk has become a major concern, leading to people living in fear. Beck believed that, in many ways, these societies have good reason to be more frightened than ever before – many of these reasons we have discussed above. As Dan Gardner states in his excellent book *Risk* (2008), however, any dispassionate reading of the data on standards of living, mortality, infant mortality, health, education and wealth allows him to conclude, 'We are the healthiest, wealthiest and longest-living people in history' but, 'we are increasingly afraid.'

The smartest brands are moving away from an interventionist paradigm and understanding that, often, brands just need to get out of the way. They no longer play on unfounded fears to create new needs but realise that they can prosper and build trust by delivering their product or service efficiently whilst having small moments of celebration with their customers in just getting the job done (see Box 5.2).

Box 5.2 Segmenting the customer for trust behaviour and experience (see Figure 5.2)

● In the language of psychology, we are acting as 'social auditors' when we make a decision to trust. Research has shown, we follow cognitive and behavioural rules that guide our decisions about people and situations. The primary cognitive rules we follow are *orientating* and *interpretation* rules.

● Orientating rules form the expectations we bring to any situation and interpretation rules help us process what has happened after we have taken action. These rules then provide us with the basis for anticipation, action and reflection in different situations.

● There are two broad strategies that take place based on these rules: we either estimate what is going to happen or take a small trusting action in order to elicit a trusting action in others and, therefore, get more information to initiate a reciprocal relationship. Of course, we often do both.

● If you want to create a trusted business and brand, it is worth understanding this process and how your customers are going to react to your trust-initiating actions. There are high and low trusters. This attitude, combined with previous experiences, will help to form segments of customers who will bring very different expectations and need different cues in order to choose to trust. They will be easier or harder to convert and have the potential to be more loyal or disloyal and cheaper or more costly to service.

● The attitude to trust or previous experiences in a category are rarely measured in consumer segments and this may form new and interesting dimensions on which to understand how likely or not it is that a customer is going to buy from your particular brand (see Figure 5.2).

How does trust work in your category?

Trust is not equal in every category, although it is essential for every product and service. The following are three key questions that can be

Figure 5.2 Different segments exist, formed by the propensity to trust and previous experiences

considered in order to work out how trust is operating within a particular category.

● Is trust operating at the functional or affective level?

In many categories, trust operates as a foundational underpinning, at the functional level, while in others it operates at a higher level – affective trust – helping to build positive and loyal relationships (see Table 5.1). Rarely, some brands can have conferred on them a level of bonded trust by some customers who come to really rely on the brand.

Table 5.1 Some examples of categories by trust level

FUNCTIONAL TRUST	AFFECTIVE TRUST	BONDED TRUST BRANDS
Credit cards	Banking	Apple
Consumer goods	Professional services	Mercedes-Benz
Automotive	Telecommunications	
Electronics		
Insurance		

● **Does trust come from the brand, the category or the system?**

From regulation to consumer bodies to standards councils – all ensure that businesses operate to a high standard that ensures safety and security. This has meant that trust in individual brands has often become a category assumption rather than a specific attribute. For example, car safety has largely become a trusted assumption for *all* car brands. Brands like Volvo, which, historically, have competed on this dimension, have therefore questioned this strategy. Recent incidents, such as the global recall of millions of vehicles by Toyota over safety concerns, will, however, challenge the category assumption of trust and make it more of a brand issue again.

● **Is or can trust be a differentiator?**

Trust is not a differentiator in many categories, but a high level of trust allows more differentiating attributes to be recognised. The John Lewis Partnership in the UK commands a high level of trust at both functional and affective levels, built on history, tradition, pricing claims ('Never knowingly undersold'), corporate structure (it is a partnership) and its relationship with customers and employees. This multilayered brand leader understands intuitively that trust underwrites all its benefits. While the shopper might not ascribe a particularly differentiated level of trust to John Lewis versus a competitor– though they might for service or quality – these attributes are built on the foundation of trust.

● **You don't know what you are promising**

Unless you understand what the balance is between risk and reward to your customer, it will be very difficult to build an ongoing trusting relationship. The move to mature understanding of the role of risk and fear, in combination with benefits, allows brands to engage on a more meaningful basis with their customers.

First Direct is a beacon brand in the UK. It was the first major bank brand to offer direct telephone banking. The power of this brand lies in the simple resolution of a tension for the customer: the convenience of direct banking through remote channels, such as the telephone or online, *and* a personal service level that is generally only found in high-end private banks. The benefit First Direct offers is convenience and service that, for the consumer, equates to saving time. The risk they manage is that, by going direct, things won't get done, with little comeback. In their best communications, they recognise both the benefit and the risk and, in so doing, create a balanced approach that commands some of the highest levels of trust for any brand in the UK.

More recently, First Direct has been winning awards for their use of social media in the form of the First Direct Live initiative. They have been integrating their social media commentary, such as Facebook and Twitter comments, into a live stream that can be seen on the First Direct website. They don't filter the results and, in not doing so, make themselves vulnerable. This is one of the best examples of a business taking a risk and, therefore, exemplifying their confidence in their ability to deliver. They are very powerfully demonstrating why we should buy from them.

Contrast this with an initiative begun by NatWest and the Royal Bank of Scotland called their Customer Charter. These brands, owned by the now nationalised RBS Group, have embarked on a multi-million-pound advertising campaign, sharing 14 commitments to make themselves the 'UK's most helpful bank'. Full of caveats and weasel words, these promises are seemingly more window-dressing than a real attempt to build trust. On the week the campaign launched, I visited five NatWest branches and no members of staff were aware of the campaign or what the impact of it was on what they should be doing.

NatWest and RBS are over-promising and we will see whether or not they will deliver, but my suspicion is that they will find it hard. They are effectively doubling their trust bet. They are not trusted now and they don't deliver good service. They know that by shouting about their intentions they will most likely change expectations in their favour. If they don't deliver, however, they will be left with even *less* trust. Perhaps they realise that their customers have so little trust in them that, ironically, they have nothing to lose!

the challenge for a trusted brand today and tomorrow is to compete based on the reality of people's experiences

Consumer understanding has always been important to the creation of great brands, but, often, it has been used to create needs that engender fear or unrealistic expectations. This was more viable in an environment of plenty and consumption. The challenge for a trusted brand today and tomorrow is to compete based on the reality of people's experiences now and their questioning of the way forwards. People want to connect and explore these new ideas together with brands that deeply understand the risk and reward of their relationship with them.

People are the heart and mind of all brands and they are more demanding and more cynical than ever. Understanding and responding to this new realism is important for brand growth in the future. We have examined these issues in this chapter and, in the next chapter, we look to see how a response to these trends can rebuild trust in brands.

TAKE ACTION TO UNDERSTAND TRUST
Look at the answers you gave to the questions in the Action box at the end of the last chapter. These will form the basis of the development of a new framework for creating trust in your brand and business.

Step 1: What are you *really* promising?
- What is the biggest risk that your customer takes by using your brand?
- What is the biggest risk your customer solves by using your brand?
- Do your promises link to the risks that you solve?
- If you promise a higher-order benefit:
  - do you really deliver
  - how
  - is your customer really buying the function or the higher benefit
  - do you compromise trust by promising higher-order benefits?

- Are your customer's needs changing to become functional and lower-order ones again?
  - What new contexts exist for these changes (environmental, health, community, family)?
- Are you creating fear or loss frames?

Step 2: What is your customer's attitude to trust?
- Do you have high-trust or low-trust customers?
- Do you understand your customer's previous experiences?
- Do you understand what your customer uses to signal trust?

Step 3: How does trust work in your category?
- Is trust mostly functional or affective or a mix?
- Where does your brand fall in the category in terms of trust?
- Is trust a differentiator in your category?
- Is there a clear trust leader in the your category?
- What is the role of system trust versus brand trust in the category?

Realities and aspirations

What you say and what you do are the cornerstones of a trusted brand. So why do so many companies fail to get their past, present and future narratives under control as they tread the line from ideal to reality to aspiration.

Language is, without doubt, the pinnacle of human evolution; it is this capacity that differentiates us from all other species. Language is the basis for our ability to exist in groups, our culture and all the achievements of humanity from art to technology. Language is linked deeply to our consciousness and it is our consciousness that allows us to trust. Consciousness gives us the ability to imagine the future and extrapolate different outcomes. This is the currency of making decisions to trust.

Human beings are social animals. Apes exhibit social behaviour, but it is relatively limited compared to that of human beings. Grooming, for example, is a social behaviour that binds groups of apes together and creates a basic form of trust and reciprocity between individuals. Language shares some of the hallmarks of grooming, but is much more efficient. Robin Dunbar (Leakey, 1994), a primatologist at University College, London, explains that, 'You can talk to several people at once and you can talk while travelling, eating or working in the fields … language evolved to integrate a larger number of individuals into their social groups.'

Our brains are full of hard-wired circuitry for understanding others' intentions and reading their minds. Mirror neurons, feedback mechanisms and hormones all programme us to link to each other using our consciousness and language in an effort to determine what

our brains are full of hard-wired circuitry for understanding others' intentions and reading their minds

will happen when we interact with others. The symbols and signals that come from this unique ability to employ complex language and create culture are the pinnacle of our achievements as a species. We have evolved to become very good at decoding these symbols and signals quickly to uncover meaning that either leads to trust or distrust. Marketing is built on these abilities.

Manipulating behaviour

Marketing is the manipulation of signals and symbols to create a change in behaviour. Companies that learn to nurture brands understand that the buy-one-get-one-free offer or 25 per cent off, may drive short-term sales, but at the expense of a long-term price premium. A perennial tension is whether or not to mortgage the value of the brand for the short-term. The creation of a long-lasting relationship with the customer based on respect and trust is the foundation of protecting this premium for the long term.

Effective delivery of the right symbols and signals is essential if we are to answer the question, 'Why should anyone buy from you?' Marketing is too often seen as a point-in-time activity with short-term aims and most brand managers have a scant regard for the history of the brands they manage. To witness the constant rebadging and rebranding that is so common nowadays is to watch rich brand heritages being destroyed.

At the core of creating an effective communication system to cultivate trust is the understanding and controlling of your business' narrative, both forwards and backwards in time. The best companies ensure that this narrative is honest, consistent and congruent and thereby commands respect and trust. Getting this right means providing the right signals and signs that help guide the customer to decide to trust easily and without lingering doubts.

The drip, drip, drip

Marketing planning is built upon 'waves'. Mostly an annual process, the marketing team will sit down to form a plan. This plan will be integrated with the new products that need to be launched, the financial targets of the company and the available resources. In most cases, these decisions will create a series of campaigns. These campaigns then become the focus of the marketing effort and become the crucible in which advertising, promotion and operational decisions are made. Promises are made to the business of cause and effect: the campaign goes out and the results come in, like a wave crashing on the shore, sweeping away all in front of it.

Unfortunately, in reality, it doesn't work like that. Building a brand is more a drip, drip, drip of slow, hard-won progression towards creating and cementing an image in people's minds. Consumers are busier and have more noise blasted at them than ever before. The competition for attention is fierce but the game we are employed in is actually cultivating rather miniscule moments of recognition. Given the wastage in the marketing system, each of these moments is expensive to win. The greatest asset a brand has is its store of these small moments of recognition in the minds of their customers or prospects.

Creating a leading brand is about fighting to get into the portfolio of brands in a consumer's mind that are not completely and utterly filtered out. As Byron Sharp describes in his brilliant book *How Brands Grow* (2010), 'We buy the same few brands over and over again and simplify buying decisions by only noticing our few regular brands ... We restrict our consideration set down to a few favoured brands.' Product quality that delivers satisfaction is now, in most categories, a given. This means that making any decision is safe and much, much easier than stressing about making a perfect choice. But at that point of purchase, have you won enough trust to get into the consideration set?

at that point of purchase, have you won enough trust to get into the consideration set?

Each of the marketing 'drips' that collect in people's minds must be honest, consistent and congruent, both in that moment and over time. Our brains work to store connections between ideas and these associations build. Good brands really do take up mindspace. Brands that constantly chop and change elements of their story are in danger of cancelling out some of their previously implanted associations or, with a mistaken message, consigning themselves to the subconscious list of brands that

good brands really do take up mindspace

an individual will never pick because of lack of awareness, previous poor experiences or just a feeling that something isn't quite right. Needless to say, once on this subconscious list, getting off it is extremely hard.

It is amazing, therefore, how few marketers take the time to really understand the past of a brand and be respectful of it as they plan. It is, I suppose, something of a consequence of the types of people who go into marketing, that they are constantly looking for the latest or new thing. Nothing could be more dangerous to the effective slow drip as consistency needs to be both strategic and tactical.

The three states of a brand

Every brand has three states: the ideal, the reality and the aspiration. This can't be avoided and it causes headaches. Research by Michael Hulme (2010), of the Institute for Advanced Studies at Lancaster University, found that 95 per cent of respondents indicated they didn't trust advertising! Only 8 per cent trust what companies say about themselves and 58 per cent agreed with the statement 'companies are only interested in selling products and services to

95 per cent of respondents indicated that they didn't trust advertising!

me, not necessarily in the product and service that is right for me.' Theodore Levitt, the author of the 1960 *Harvard Business Review* classic *Marketing Myopia*, would be turning in his grave! We are clearly going wrong somewhere.

Advertising always, almost by definition, is based on the *ideal* of a brand – it is the best representation of the company, the product and the service. Given that it always excludes any flaws or issues, when we know there *must* be some, it only represents half the story. This is compounded when the promises are elevated on to the astral plane of 'self-actualisation', where over-claiming is the norm.

The reality of a business or product is always quite different from the ideal experience. Given the huge number of variables from product design to delivery that are out of the control of most companies, this is almost always true. Every brand also has aspirations. Most businesses want to get to a better or different place. They want to build on what they have but improve and strive for more. So how can we reconcile these states?

This can be attempted by controlling the signals that we give to the customer, by tightly orchestrating the narrative and telling compelling stories. Activities need to support the achievement of the ideal – not be too out of touch with the reality – and provide a framework for moving towards the aspiration. Brands also need to ensure that they have the infrastructure and an answer in place to handle the numerous situations when the ideal promised in the advertising doesn't match up to the reality.

This reconciliation can be achieved most easily by telling a compelling story that has momentum. Gerzema and Lebar in *The Brand Bubble* (2008) call this 'Energy' and some of the brands they have analysed as having momentum are Amazon, Virgin, Innocent, Google, Vodafone and GE, among others. These brands, in general, have a clear mission, set of values, strong leadership and the drive to achieve. This momentum carries the customer through the different states, buys forgiveness when things go wrong and creates a forward-leaning orientation towards a better aspiration. If the customer goes on this journey, then it is a powerful basis for trusting and profitable relationships.

momentum carries the customer through the different states, buys forgiveness when things go wrong and creates a forward-leaning orientation

Matching the brand signals with brand reality

Two leading Oxford University professors of social science – Michael Bacharach and Diego Gambetta (2001) – have done much thinking about games theory and trust signalling. They invented a trust concept of 'krypta and manifesta' to explore how trust-givers and takers can judge each other in a transaction.

Krypta are the actual qualities of a person and I will extend this to the actual qualities of businesses and their brands. *Manifesta* are the observed signals that are seen or experienced by the trust-giver, the customer, to decide whether or not someone, or a brand, is trustworthy.

The role of marketing, then, is to ensure that there is alignment between the *krypta* (what the product actually does, how the service is, what the company is really up to) and the *manifesta* (the proposition, product claims, service delivery, pricing, advertising). The role of advertising in this model is to present to the customer the most favourable krypta by making a show of the manifesta. The first manifesta is achieved by just turning up to the advertising party – you have something to say.

Advertising works in part because it is an extravagant waste of money. This extravagance is a clear signal to the customer that the organisation can afford to 'waste' its resources and, therefore, is of a size and scale to be of importance and worthy of consideration. Rory Sutherland, chairman of the advertising agency Ogilvy & Mather and chairman of the IPA, sums this up nicely: 'Advertising is like a peacock's tail. The peacock has evolved this tail with its luxurious colours and size as an extravagant addition so that it can signal to the female that it is strong and healthy enough to survive whilst having such a wasteful appendage.'

Despite the benefit of just making a bet on the poker table of advertising, the messaging and signalling turns just an oversized bunch of feathers into something beautiful and mesmerising to behold. Effective signalling

– especially if a brand is to command trust – comes from ensuring that your krypta are aligned with your manifesta. It might work once to promise something attractive and then not deliver, but it is not a sustainable strategy. Achieving close alignment is the way to being seen as trustworthy.

The trouble is that most brand strategies and variations on vision, mission, values or principles usually don't represent the reality of what is actually driving the company forwards. When working as a consultant for a very large communications company that was rolling out a new vision, mission and set of values, I remember this incongruity being made very clear to me. This particular company was a collection of acquisitions and, therefore, my consultancy had been brought in to develop a coherent view of what the business should and could stand for. The strategy had been signed off by the board after much wrangling and the brochures printed, the presentations written and we were now in rollout mode.

Everyone was excited as the first 200 employees poured into a hall to hear their leaders unveil the widely anticipated new direction for the firm. The statements were full of fantastic (in more ways than one) concepts of trust, innovation, customer service, technology and treating employees well. The presentation was well received and we were all pleased. I wandered outside the hall and overheard two attendees chatting, one saying to the other, 'That's all very nice but I thought we were here to make money.' His comment has stayed with me for the rest of my career and certainly changed my approach to working out what a business should stand for.

that's all very nice but I thought we were here to make money

To illustrate the point further, I looked at the companies in the FTSE 100 and their visions or missions or purposes. Three things strike you. First they are often hard to find, second they are mostly written in buzzwords that only vaguely make sense and, most strikingly, very few mention the making of money. Now I'd wager that the top management teams of all these companies spend more time obsessing about their earnings and profits than 'magical customer service' or 'enhanced technology innovation'. Rarely do you find a purpose that actually is written in down-to-earth language that gets at the core of what the company is trying to do, which is deliver a service and make a fair return. This signals a misaligned krypta and manifesta. When these signals are aligned with the true drives of the company, this becomes an enabler of delivery. Two examples of good purposes are WPP:

> *To develop and manage talent; to apply that talent, throughout the world, for the benefit of clients; to do so in partnership; to do so with profit.*

and Tesco:

> *Our core purpose is to create value for customers to earn their lifetime loyalty.*
> *Our success depends on people: the people who shop with us and the people who work with us. If our customers like what we offer, they are more likely to come back and shop with us again. If the Tesco team find what we do rewarding, they are more likely to go that extra mile to help our customers.*

It is hard to build or maintain trust when the writing on the wall, literally, is divorced from the day-to-day reality of what is happening in the business. It creates a sense of dislocation within the organisation and, in doing so, compromises the ability to achieve the ideal and deal with the reality while moving towards the aspiration. The most congruent businesses have this nut cracked, but there aren't many of them.

Strategies to signal trustworthiness

Aphasia and agnosia are two brain disorders that affect the way that language is processed. They result most often from brain damage to different parts of the brain that deal with language. Aphasia affects the right temporal lobe and is an inability to understand language and, specifically, the meanings of words. Agnosia affects the left temporal lobe and is where words can be *understood*, but they are stripped of all other expression, such as tone, feeling or character.

Remarkably, both aphasics and agnosics can cope with their condition quite well, as their other faculties almost miraculously compensate. I first came across descriptions of these conditions in Oliver Sacks' book on brain disorders, *The Man Who Mistook his Wife for a Hat* (1985). He describes patients with aphasia and agnosia watching a president's inaugural speech. Both groups could understand quite well the communication, even though some could understand none of the *words* but all of the *signals*, while others understood *only* the words, stripped of all other signals.

The aphasic patients understand without words and use purely cadence, body language and nuance to decode what is being said. Sacks says it is impossible to lie to an aphasic because they cannot be deceived by your words. The agnosics, though, understand by analysing the structure and logic of what is being said. They have little context and, therefore, can only rely on the words, their order and the logic of the argument. Both groups can understand reasonably well one group forensically analysing the krypta and the other the manifesta.

Communication is both *what* is said and *how* it is said. Advertising folks readily understand and employ this. When communication works, it uses words, meanings and symbols to meet the needs of both the aphasics and the agnosics.

communication is both *what* is said and *how* it is said

Sociological research into signalling strategies between trust-givers and trust-takers has identified that there are four main signalling strategies that can be employed to communicate trustworthiness (see also Box 6.1). They work by increasing the cognitive cost of withdrawing from the emerging relationship and reducing the trust-giver's perceived risk of being exploited. They can, of course, be employed singly or in concert.

The four strategies are

- showing commitment
- congruence and consistency
- demonstrating competence
- signalling integrity.

SHOWING COMMITMENT

Marketing plays with commitment frequently. When analysed in the context of a trust exchange, promotions and even advertising itself are forms of commitment. Promotions give something to the customer 'for nothing'. 'Peacock investments' in advertising are, again, seen by the consumer as a significant commitment. When a piece of advertising entertains or touches an emotion, it is a kind of gift from the brand to the viewer. These actions work because they initiate the powerful expectation of reciprocity. They increase the cost of pulling out of a potential transaction by effectively giving something to the potential customer, which then creates the subconscious expectation of needing to give something back in return. In many cases, the commitment strategy can be risky because it exacts cost in its refusal. It is painful, for example, to throw the kitchen designer out from your house once he or she has spent two hours doing you a design 'for free', but then wants to close the deal there and then. To resist reciprocity is difficult indeed.

CONGRUENCE AND CONSISTENCY

If you have studied and still believe in neuro-linguistic programming (NLP), you may be aware of your 'congruent signal'. NLP teaches you to find and understand that particular feeling we all get when we feel something isn't intuitively right. For me, it is a knot in the pit of my stomach and I feel it when I get a sense that something isn't going right. Incongruence is a massive contributor to a lack of trust. Like the car salesperson pushing a particular car too hard or you ringing the bank, only to be kept on hold for ten minutes, these situations fire off reactions that form negative associations in your brain, making it harder to trust.

The important elements of the congruence strategy are to communicate signs that suggest a matching of qualities, values and ways of acting between the brand and the potential customer. This signals that the customer can make good judgements and form their expectations solidly. Using celebrities in advertising plays the congruence game by giving a face to the brand that presents easily understood signals and allows human connections to form.

Congruence over time, or consistency, is also a big contributor to this strategy. As has been aptly demonstrated many times, consistency is less about names and logos and more about delivery. Marathon to Snickers, Midland Bank to HSBC, Bounty to Plenty – these changes matter little to the consumer. Much more serious is the product and service quality that underlies them. Get a mouldy Snickers and that association will stick.

When a brand attempts something that is incongruent, it can go badly wrong. When British Airways decided to change its corporate identity in the 1990s, it got into significant trouble. The strategy was perhaps sound on paper: the world is globalising, we have a British and imperial heritage, surely we can be seen as a brand with British values with global appeal? By changing the tail fins of all its planes from the Union Jack to symbols from around the world, however, a significant signal of incongruence was created with its core audience and so BA quick high-tail-finned it back to the red, white and blue.

DEMONSTRATING COMPETENCE

This strategy is the most common in advertising campaigns and attempts to place the brand or business between the problem and customer. The brand signals trustworthiness because it presents itself as being in control of a situation that is uncontrollable for the customer. Brands as diverse as antibacterial cleaning brands to financial services providers employ this strategy.

The strategy is much more effective when the brand's efficacy can be demonstrated in a concrete way. Traditionally, this has been achieved through claims: 'kills 99 per cent of germs dead', or 'makes your hair 58 per cent stronger' or even 'working to help our clients since 1856' – all are competence-based claims. Most consumer goods companies have realised that claims are most effective when they are unquantifiable by the consumer ('How do you tell if your hair is 58 per cent stronger?') rather than easily auditable.

SIGNALLING INTEGRITY

The integrity strategy is the most difficult to get right and has high levels of potential risk, but also a big pay-off because, ultimately, the highest level of trust comes from rock solid, unshakeable integrity. Not all brands have the option to employ it convincingly. There have been painful recent examples where brands employing this strategy have become unstuck. The integrity strategy was employed by most major banks prior to the recent financial collapse. Most have now moved away to employ other strategies. For example, UBS changed from its long-standing theme of 'You and us', an integrity claim, to 'We will not rest', which is much more of a commitment claim.

Box 6.1 The trouble with aspirations
An interview with Mark Ritson, associate professor of marketing, Melbourne Business School

I've known Mark Ritson for years, from his early days teaching brand management at the London Business School. His weekly column in *Marketing Week* should be a highlight of every marketer's week and certainly is mine. He has an uncanny ability to sniff out the oh-so-common absurdities of brand marketing and pulls no punches in exposing them. There are relatively few people in business who actually understand the real reasons why we do something, especially in the marketing space, and have the ability to take the long view, but Mark is one of them.

'We easily forget that there was a period, say in the nineteenth and early twentieth centuries, when trusting a company was almost

---

impossible, even bizarre. Applying anthropomorphic concepts to companies is second nature to us in the twenty-first century, but it would have been completely hilarious in earlier times. The question, "Do your customers trust the brand" just wouldn't have made sense to Mr Johnson, a 1920s bank manager. We are now much more comfortable applying love or relationship or trust to companies. We should remember that these are concepts drawn from the human relationship rather than the corporate one.' Mark paused to take a drink.

'It's the postmodern condition that allows us to treat companies as if they were humans and humans as if they were commodities.' This is profound for me, but I'm keen to learn more about how Mark thinks about trust.

'Trust is an anticipation that you will get the emotional and rational benefits that have been promised. Trust is fundamental glue, the conveyor belt of delivery. It has a shorter half-life now and is acyclical.'

We talk some more and then I ask why do so many brand-positioning work and company statements do not include any reference to making money, to the commercial aims of the organisation.

'The word "aspirational" is used far too much and is an excuse to ignore reality. "Aspirational" has come to dominate brand-positioning exercises and this has led, often, to flights of fancy that over-promise and under-deliver and destroy trust. In terms of trust, aspirational means don't be honest with the customer in terms of what you do, how you make money and what you deliver, but focus instead on a series of totally hopeless words that mean very little,' the energy in Mark's voice is palpable as he rises to his theme.

'It's only the best marketers, unfortunately, who truly realise that you have to be trustworthy – and that means based in reality, because to be trusted makes you more money. Brands and marketing are at their best when they catalyse some ongoing societal and cultural change. That is when marketing is at its most potent. In order to do this, a brand must be trusted to drive the change. It's not a differentiator but a vital ingredient in any business that wants to make an impact on its market.'

The story matters

One of the most powerful consequences of the human evolution of language has been the ability to tell stories. Good storytelling is at the heart of communication, but many marketers and their advertising agencies, at the behest of short-term targets, don't pay enough attention to the narrative and its control over time. A brand's narrative is rich and comes at consumers from different angles. Unlike the silo structure of businesses, people don't differentiate when they come across an advert or read the financial pages or see a CEO getting paid vast sums – it all gets filed under that brand in the brain. Most companies, though, rarely manage all these streams of external narrative into the market consistently or coherently. When a brand does, it can be extremely powerful.

Super-brands, such as Apple or Nike, and their leaders are on top of their narrative and this allows them to stage manage their messaging for fantastic impact, loyalty and cost-effectiveness. They can use this narrative in new ways to connect on deeper issues. Nike for example is championing the use of sport in adolescent girls' lives in the developing world through the Nike Foundation. The 'girl effect' was a piece of communication that went viral and created connections on deeper issues between Nike and people. Nike had the bravery to take a point of view and the resources to make a difference and those actions create trust. This then becomes a richer part of its narrative.

An audit of a brand's past, present and future can help the organisation become aware of the consistency and congruency of the message that it needs to deliver. Marketers should be at least as aware of the history of the brand as they are of the current plans for achieving targets and business goals.

marketers should be at least as aware of the history of the brand as they are of the current plans

This doesn't just apply to brands with a long heritage. Innocent is a brand of fruit smoothies that has developed its narrative extremely effectively in a consistent and congruent fashion to create a hugely profitable brand leader in a little under ten years. The narrative of Innocent is about how the brand was founded by 'mere' boys who had a great product and a dream. The company has used this narrative smartly to create a clear set of associations. These associations are slightly naïve and innocent in their intention, as if the founders had just happened upon the idea of trying to create something good for you that tasted 'yummy'. There is no mention of the fact that the founders were mainly ex-management consulting types and, therefore, I am sure, had business plans and financial forecasts coming out of their ears. They weren't the first smoothies, but they were the first to create significant mindspace and, therefore, reap the rewards of getting a new category of drink on the consideration set of their customers.

Innocent's story is not without some incongruence, though. In 2009, it decided to sell some of the equity in the company to Coca-Cola. This created a reasonable amount of negative publicity and questioning about its intentions and if Coke was the right partner. It got through it, but not without considerable PR and some consumer backlash. There are now cracks appearing in Innocent's brand reality. It is in dispute over its brand design with a brand of vitamins and moving into segments of the market, such as orange juice, that seem to have more to do with growth than its brand journey. Overall, it feels like the brand has peaked and carries less authenticity and trust than before.

Creating and running a successful brand is a complex dance of expectations management and delivery. All of this involves processes being gone through by people over time and, too often, brands are quick to change and slow to regret, throwing the baby out with the bath water. There are only a few that succeed over a long period, but, for those that do, a treasured place in their customers lives is the prize.

In the next chapter, we look at how communications models in companies need to fundamentally change and be realigned with the new tools that people are using to communicate and connect.

TAKE ACTION TO SIGNAL TRUST

Step 1: Audit your signals and narrative over the long term
- Pull together all the communications that your business has issued over the long term (ideally ten years, if not longer).
- Be as comprehensive as you can: work with colleagues from PR and investor relations, plus your agencies.
- Analyse the timeline for the following (if you can't do it internally, show the timeline to some outsiders and ask them to recall what they took out from the timeline or ask a new recruit with a fresh set of eyes to do the project):
  – themes and storylines
  – benefits and risks
  – signals
  – shocks.

Step 2: Compare the audit with the internal reality
- Pull together the internal narrative (if you can't do it yourself, then interview people around the company) for the same period.
- Look for changes in leadership, new missions, values statements, new product launches, significant external events, significant changes in internal policy (for example, new performance management or incentive systems). Be sure to include financial performance and internal culture measures if available.
- Analyse the timeline for the same dimensions as Step 1.
- Compare the output of internal and external messaging and look for consistency, congruence and commitment to the customer.

Step 3: Invent the future
- Imagine you are ten years in the future and perform the same exercise again
- What would you want the analysis to say against the core elements in order to create the most trusted brand in your category?
- How can you take advantage of the major trends in customer needs, attitudes and transparency to achieve your business goals?
- How can you form deeper connections with your customers through co-creation?
- How does this tie in with the corporate strategy, vision and values and the internal reality of the business today? Is it aligned with the vision of the business' leadership?

Step 4: Assess the impact
- What needs to change?
  - How does your marketing strategy need to change?
  - How does your business strategy need to change?
  - How does your internal culture need to change?
  - How does the business leadership need to change?

The turning point

People power is wreaking havoc with the establishment way of communicating. Access to information and connectedness is rewriting the rules of the game and creating a battle for the voice of business.

Being a peasant in England in 1480 was filthy and dismal. The dirt poor resided in dirty houses with vermin crawling everywhere. Everything and everyone stank. People got married in June because yearly baths were in May. It was believed that the stench in the air carried disease and so, to cover the smell and ward off illness, brides and many of the rich, carried posies of flowers. Despite a small population, graveyards often ran out of space for the dead; the life expectancy was no higher than mid-thirties. The devastating pandemic of the Black Death was still in recent memory. Whole villages and towns had been wiped out by this terrible disease. Two million deaths from an English population of six million meant every family had been affected.

Society was basic, and as a peasant, you would most likely have been in servitude to a local lord. Community life was parochial and insular, but loyalty, even in adverse situations, to this community was strong and lasting. Generations were kept in the servitude of a particular nobleman or order. God was extremely important to the hard life that was lived in these communities. The unambiguous goal of an involvement in the Church was salvation. Hence, the Church's role in society was massively important. As mediators for an all-powerful and authoritarian God, the priesthood was powerful.

Individuality was not a common concept – ordinary people were part of the collective, controlled by the landed, the State and the Church. Life was grim, but it was better lived together than as an individual. You did what you were told. Choice was rare. Life, while unpleasant, was at least predictable.

Change was afoot, however. New levels of connectivity and innovations in information technology would help create and propagate ideas that would have a profound effect on the lives of ordinary people. Over the next 100 years or so, the dominance of the Catholic Church would wane, millions would die in wars, some of the greatest art and music would be created and new political and community structures would be established that still cast an influence over our world today.

In the republics of Florence and Venice, scholars of the classic Latin texts were rediscovering the Greek philosophers. New connections were being made in these cities as people and ideas converged. Great minds such as Petrarch, Salutati, de' Niccoli and Bracciolini were challenging the existing thinking about society, law, economics and hierarchy. Great artists such as Leonardo da Vinci, Botticelli and Michelangelo found patronage from the Florentine banker Lorenzo d'Medici to make their ideas a reality. A new framework to process these new ideas was arising. Humanism – a process of discovery based on evidence and empirical study – brought an exciting idea that humankind was 'genius', with unique and extraordinary abilities.

This humanist approach created an idea that is still influencing our world now – that of people as individuals rather than as part of a collective. In cities, people started to break away from single associations, either spurning them completely or becoming more plural. New religious orders were founded as people became frustrated with the constant political disagreements and conflicts between the leadership of states and the Church. The building blocks of our collective store of social capital were being formed.

Religion wasn't the only thing to change. New forms of political and secular organisation were appearing. Martin Luther's Reformation theology, spread through the latest in communications technology – the printing press, proposed a realignment of the individual in relation to God that started a revolution. Local communities were becoming more hierarchical and ordered so that law and order and communal assets could be maintained. Order was being applied to taxation, policing and military recruitment. Individuals were becoming the focus of many of the

State policies – with the movement from communal taxation to individual taxes, for example.

Education and social welfare were becoming more commonplace and had to be funded. In totality, these changes presented a painful and often lethal situation for the majority. Structures in which people had maintained their trust and a sense of the world were being weakened and, in many cases, dismantled. There was a deep sense of dislocation from the past and uncertainty about the future. Suddenly an ill-educated man could not rely on the ritual sacrifice or sacred talisman as a route to salvation, but now had to delve deeply into his soul and purse.

Less crisis and more reformation

We are at a turning point, now – much like Europe in the Middle Ages. New connectivity, new technology and access to capital are leading to new ideas and new questions. Pressing issues that threaten our survival – or at least our ability to thrive in the ways we have been used to – are challenging us. Our available store of social capital is diminishing as we deal with so many changes and challenges at once and we feel a sense of dislocation. This dislocation is both a threat and an opportunity for businesses and brands in answering the question, 'Why should anyone buy from you?'

Just as technology in the form of the printing press caused a discontinuity in the connectivity and contagion of ideas that led, at least in part, to the huge upheaval of the Reformation, the Internet is doing the same for us. Technology brings huge benefits, but, just as it did 500 years ago and many times since, it also brings threats.

the gap brings with it deep-seated frustration between what we are starting to suspect needs to change and the solutions available to us

We are living through 'the gap' and this feels unsettling. The gap is what happens when access to information and ideas outstrips the ability for structures in society, government, business and organisations, to respond with change (see Figure 7.1). The gap in the 1500s created profound shifts in the major power structures of the time, namely the Church. Now the gap brings with it deep-seated frustration between what we are starting to suspect needs to change and the solutions available to us.

The gap can be seen in many places today: in the attitude to politicians and democracy, now untrusted and seen as self-serving but slow to change; in an economy based on conspicuous consumption and the promise of never-ending growth that has been divorced from any concept of anything real. The gap can be seen in businesses that exploit resources for the good of shareholders and short-term gain rather than sustainable profit for all stakeholders. All of these gaps are connected to a planet that is precariously balanced as demand outstrips supply. The gap surrounds us. We have an increasing understanding of the problems, but seemingly little in the way of solutions.

Figure 7.1 The gap that occurs when access to information and ideas outpaces the ability of structures to change in response

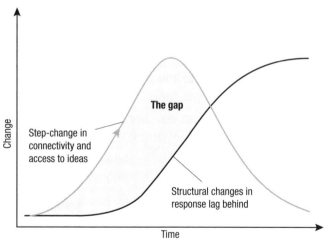

From mass communications to mass interactions

The Reformation was caused by the spread of a new theology that had, at its heart, the centrality of individual access to God, which put us on a path from a collective existence to individuality that, I believe, had its denouement in the Western free market capitalism of the past 30 years. We are now at an inflexion point where new forms of collective living are appearing that use our communications technology not to broadcast top-down messages but foster new connections.

We are now living in an age of mass *interaction*, not mass *communication*. There has always been a symbiosis between the development of media and marketing. Advertising money paid for, and still pay for, mass communication channels. From advertising in newspapers in the early part of the last century to the soap operas and TV advertising after World War II through to the Internet today – all this has been paid for by marketing.

The game is changing now from eyeballs to engagement and from attention to contention. The currency of advertising in the mass communications paradigm is largely, although it is changing, the delivery of audiences (that is, eyeballs) and how much people notice a particular message (that is, attention). Advertising focuses on optimising whether a message is memorable, appealing and credible. Media focuses on optimising opportunity to view and repetition, targeting a particular audience and conversion. The Internet fundamentally challenged these existing paradigms of how to use communications to build connections and start the trust-building process (see also Box 7.1).

the game is changing now from eyeballs to engagement and from attention to contention

Box 7.1 The communications model is changing

An interview with Cathryn Sleight, marketing director at Unilever and former marketing director at Coca-Cola, UK

'We had never proved the exact relationship between brand and corporate reputation and market share, but we knew intuitively that it was important and trust was key', said Cathryn Sleight, talking about her time at Coca-Cola.

'We embarked on a joint project to analyse and develop a model for trust in our brands and trust in the reputation of the corporation. Both corporate affairs and marketing worked hand-in-hand co-dependently to achieve an answer. What we found was that trust was essential to our success.'

It is fascinating learning from a marketer who has succeeded in some of the biggest brand environments. I ask, how is consumer behaviour changing the landscape of trust?

'Consumers are more curious and inquisitive than ever. They have access to more and more information, pulling it towards them and making connections. They easily make links and form their own opinions about the brands and corporations they buy from. Consumer concern around sustainability in the broad sense means they are more interested in forming a bigger picture of a brand's practices and impact', says Cathryn.

I ask about the Internet and communities of interest, since much of Cathryn's work has been with brands that invest successfully and heavily in digital marketing.

'Brands are, at some level, just communities of interest and, with the Internet, it's become so much easier to harness these communities to allow new connections to be formed. It's essential that externally facing departments work together co-dependently to ensure the right outcome and joined-up thinking. It doesn't matter what the structure is, but to succeed in today's communication – and information-rich environment, departments must work together with the same outcomes in mind', answers Cathryn.

'How is the communications model changing?' I interject.

'The communications model is definitely changing. Communications needs to be much more joined up than in the past. Transparency and openness are keys to success – you can't hide any more. Many more people have influence over your brand than in the past. The consumer, employees, the media – all work to adapt perceptions both positively and negatively. Being able to navigate this landscape is where the best brands will gain advantage.'

From eyeballs to engagement

Is it better to get 1,000,000 to have the opportunity to see your marketing or 1000 to engage with it? Where should you focus – on the 1,000,000 or the 1000? This, simply put, is the challenge in the planning of most marketing today. Those with significant resources will do both, but the vast majority of the money spent, if not the effort, will go on delivering the 1,000,000. What this has created, as media has fragmented, got cheaper and more accessible to more businesses, is the exponential rise in advertising. According to ZenithOptimedia, the global media-buying and planning business, global advertising spend was nearly half a trillion dollars in 2010 – and this doesn't include many aspects of marketing, such as promotion. Now advertising is ubiquitous, from YouTube to urinals. For the consumer there is far too much – people are overwhelmed and overloaded. Optimising for the 1,000,000 creates a paradigm of waste.

is it better to get 1,000,000 to have the opportunity to see your marketing or 1,000 to engage with it?

The game, facilitated by the Internet and increasingly mobile devices, is engagement – optimising for the 1000, not the 1,000,000. The currency of this approach is less the *mass* audience and more the *engaged* audience. In the end, there are really only three types of customer: the engaged, the temporarily engaged and the 'just do your job and get out of my way', with the mix of these being more category-dependent rather than brand dependent than most businesses will admit. Understanding how to build trust with each of these groups can unlock insight (see Table 7.1).

The largest group is almost always the 'just do your job and get out of my way' group. These customers have high levels of functional trust and low levels of affective trust; they neither want nor care about having a relationship with the brand. For these customers, the product or service needs to work reliably, honestly and without any negatives.

Those in the engaged group want to have a relationship with the brand at both a functional and an affective level. The engaged customer is one who trusts consciously. He or she will explore and even co-create with the brands they have this relationship with. When something goes wrong – like a product defect or recall – it is the engaged customer who both sharply criticises the company to its face and also defends it to others. This is the classic behaviour of advocates of the Apple brand. Blog after blog of engaged Apple customers will criticise when the iPhone has an issue, discussing and berating openly *within* the community, but they will still sing the virtues of the brand to others outside the inner circle.

The engaged are important to a brand or business because we are programmed through evolution to copy. Imitation is a much more effective evolutionary strategy than experimentation. Trying new things, such as a new food or a new way of hunting, will always have a higher cost than just watching others and copying. The engaged talk about their brand experiences and others follow.

the floating voter ... can often be the most important to understand and capture

The last group – the temporarily engaged – most often get forgotten. The floating voter, the undecided, the 'don't know' – this group can often be the most important to understand and capture. Often with this group, something has happened to cause their brief, fleeting

Table 7.1 Different groups need different approaches to building trust.

		ENGAGEMENT AND CREDIBILITY	SETTING AND UNDERSTANDING EXPECTATIONS	HONESTY AND RESPECTFULNESS	KEEPING COMMITMENTS AND CONSISTENCY	TRUSTING AND BEING TRUSTWORTHY
THE ENGAGED	Functional and affective trust	Create together the brand's narrative	Explore and define boundaries	Demonstrate through quality interactions and listening	Co-create the boundary commitments with consistency of approach	Take opportunities through interaction to demonstrate
THE TEMPORARILY ENGAGED	Functional and, for a time affective trust	Use the brand's narrative	Define and be clear on expectations and their prior experience	Give the right information to help restore the status quo quickly	Understand both benefit and risk	Create moments of truth to demonstrate
'JUST DO YOUR JOB AND GET OUT OF MY WAY'	Functional trust	Deliver in a way that allows me to trust and forget	Allow this group to not have relationships and just be purchasers	Just be straightforward and simple	Guarantee product quality/ delivery	Deliver and ensure that, when things go wrong, recovery is good

engagement with the product, but trust has broken down, often through product or service issues, causing them to reassess their decision. A competitive brand then has an in.

Temporary engagement can be promoted in a category by perturbing the equilibrium by creating new elements and ideas. A new format, a new benefit or a quality issue can all create a higher level of temporary engagement, but the status quo will be re-established. Fast-moving consumer goods play this game well, with almost constant 'innovation', introducing new formats – liquids to powdered detergents or shower gel to replace soap, for example. Ariel's campaign 'Turn down to 30°' was a good example of a brand competing with new, consumer-relevant benefits that caused the customer to ask a new question of their brands.

The elements of trust are all applicable to each of these groups, but in different ways. Table 7.1 describes how each element of trust can be developed or used with these groups.

From attention to contention

How do you ensure attention in today's crowded marketplace? Is it enough just to present a product's qualities to a consumer in order to answer the question, 'Why should anyone buy from you?'

For decades, marketing and advertising have relied on repetition of a message to ensure that the idea goes into potential consumer's heads. In a world where people have many more tools to filter out these repetitive messages, however, new approaches need to be worked out.

When Dove developed their mould-breaking 'Real women', campaign, they exploited a powerful argument around images of beauty and made a contribution to the debate. When Nike invest millions in sport for young women because it is proven to boost self-esteem and a positive self-image, they are taking a point of view in an important series of societal issues. Even BP, as they rebranded, redefining themselves as 'Beyond petroleum', were seeking to engage in the debate over the future of energy. All these brands have moved into potentially contentious arguments to help define their brands and present their voice in the debate.

Successful brands today are taking the risk to engage in debate with people. Contention is a powerful route to engagement. The debate that is entered into, however, must be authentic, real and meaningful. Some brands try to create debate around issues that are important to them but almost no one else: how many people are really going to engage meaningfully with, say, what sandwich filling is best on a Monday? Those brands that pick meaningful debates and contribute authentic thinking to the mixing pot will have a great chance of being trusted.

successful brands today are taking the risk to engage in debate with people

The battle for the voice of business

There is a battle raging in most corporations today. The battleground is the Internet and social media and the weapons are transparency and connectedness. CEOs sitting in their tents are like the kings of old and their PR or communications advisers are their generals. Their battle plan is simple: control the hierarchy employing the big guns of advertising, press releases, corporate websites, interviews and other forms of proclamation in the town square.

The enemy being fought is the millions of messages and communications between customers, employees and prospects, magnified and captured forever electronically. The enemy is unstructured and guerrilla in its tactics, not operating according to any established rules, and self-organising. Some of those who are the enemy have an agenda, others don't. Most don't even know they are taking part in the battle. The generals also know that the enemy is within.

CEOs and their PR generals have already lost the battle, although most still don't realise it and almost none know what to do about it. They are locked in an old paradigm: most corporates monitor the Web as they do traditional media and are petrified of engaging with it. The policies of most corporates forbid their employees to say anything about work and what is happening in the company or at least seek to control what they say. CEOs of the biggest companies crumble in the face of a crisis, defeated by exposure to the views of so many people. Witness Tony Hayward, erstwhile CEO of BP, making gaffs such as his now notorious comment, 'I want my life back', while dealing with the worst environmental disaster in US history where 11 workers lost *their* lives.

CEOs and generals have already lost the battle, although most still don't realise it and almost none knows what to do about it

Top-down is dead

Most communications strategies in companies are top-down: the CEO or a small cadre of top managers are permitted to speak on a defined range of topics. They can filter messages down through the organisation and outwards to external audiences (see Figure 7.2). They are tutored and drilled in how to communicate and deliver the 'right' messages by media trainers and advisers.

Everyone else is given a general set of guidelines as to what they can and can't say. In most cases, making external comments is forbidden, which, given the rise in social media, presents a problem. Is a pronouncement on Facebook about having 'a good day' or even 'a terrible day', a public comment on the company? One poor employee found out that complaining about 'a crap boss' *is* a public comment and was sacked for it. Similarly, my blog and website (www.basini.com) got written up in an internal audit of my marketing department when I worked for a large corporation for breaching some of the rules on sharing information. My offence was that I had shared a presentation from a conference and I

Figure 7.2 The top-down communications paradigm is being replaced by a side-to-side peer-to-peer approach

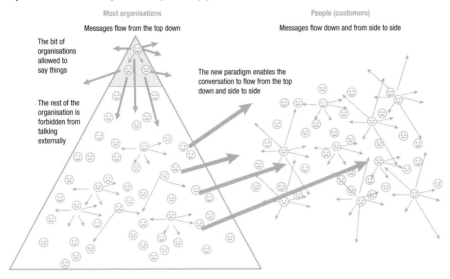

had overlooked removing the footer proclaiming it was 'proprietary and confidential', even though the content wasn't. I'll leave it to you to judge how serious this was and whether or not it was worth the hours of people's time it took writing it up, assessing it for risk and discussing it.

The top-down communications model is dying and being replaced by a new paradigm empowering and trusting people to communicate. The future of communications – creating engagement – will happen by allowing employees to engage in the conversation. The biggest assets that a brand has in communication are not its media budgets, the advertising agencies or the press releases, but its people. Unleashing employees to carry the conversation forwards is powerful because it is authentic, spontaneous and fundamentally more trustworthy. It is also highly challenging to the way that corporations and most brands think about communications today because it is largely uncontrollable and messy.

unleashing employees to carry the conversation forwards is powerful because it is authentic

The reason that Tony Hayward, CEO of BP, or Akio Toyoda, CEO of Toyota, or Fred Goodwin, ex-CEO of the Royal Bank of Scotland, aren't effective as corporate spokespeople any more is that the normal man on the street trusts them very little, if at all and certainly doesn't identify with them, no longer even respecting them.

In his first interview following the Gulf of Mexico disaster, Tony Hayward said, 'You know, it's very difficult to hate a company, it's much easier to hate an individual', but this misses the point. People don't hate the *ordinary* man or woman working for BP; they hate these men who live in a rarefied world of the corporate super league and have almost nothing to do with normal life. They don't talk in normal language and they don't have normal experiences. They are seen as the self-serving top dogs in businesses whose ability is to turn a profit or have a good CSR policy.

The people working for them, however – often tens of thousands of people – are our next-door neighbours, fellow parents at the local school, people we go to church or the pub with. We trust them because they are us, but too often, they are told they can't talk about their life at work or have to trot out the corporate line for fear that they are betraying their company or breaching their contract.

Toyota realised this in the UK when they suffered issues with the safety of many of their popular vehicles, causing the recall of thousands of them. A slow start in the company's response saw them default to the standard modus operandi of big companies in crisis mode: rolling out their senior management to do interviews. This was patchy in its success. Toyota learned quickly, however, developing a strategy that harnessed their people and social media, as well as traditional advertising, to shore up their position. They created message boards and Twitter streams and a series of videos detailing the company's response. Toyota explained their actions in terms of how hard they were working *as a team* to respond to the issues. It is easy to be suspicious of a suited and booted CEO, probably paid far too much to sit on the couch of BBC Breakfast News, but it is a whole lot easier to sympathise and value the work of 2000 people, from mechanics to customer service agents, working very hard to make a bad situation good again.

Unleash the people

I am not advocating that employees are completely left to their own devices – there needs to a set of guidelines that regulate employee contributions in talking about the businesses with which they work. Intellectual property and personnel confidentialities must be maintained, but most corporate policies reserve rights far beyond this.

We've discussed how the brands that will win in this emerging paradigm will have real and meaningful sets of values that reflect what the business is there to achieve and guide its people in pursuit of these goals. This must become the over-arching guideline for how people are to behave. Within these norms of behaviour, people should be encouraged to talk and engage with their friends and family outside the company, to discuss what is going on and freely give their perspective. The best companies will find ways to learn from these interactions systematically and harvest the knowledge and insight that surfaces.

As a last example, let's turn to the Royal Bank of Scotland Group. They have fallen from an aggressively growing financial services group, able to swallow the huge parts of ABM Amro in the biggest banking takeover in history, to effective bankruptcy and collapse, being forced into State ownership.

Talking with insiders, the internal cultural journey is fascinating. The RBS Group, like many banks, was a loose collection of fiefdoms – more a federacy than an integrated unit – and, as such, had little in the way of a central values set, vision or mission. The cultures therefore differed, from the trading floor in the City to the branches up and down the country.

As the dust settled from the collapse, top management decided that there needed to be a much clearer sense of purpose, values and culture to the Group. Lots of advice was sought from expensive consultants and a committee of top management was formed to decide what the values should be. I am sure much research, again at considerable expense, was completed that identified what the different constituencies, from employees to customers to shareholders, thought. Decisions were made and the new statements were formulated. This is top-down communication and decision making in action.

Why didn't RBS choose 'another way'? What an opportunity for this nationalised business to engage their many thousands of employees in a dialogue with the nation about what banks should be doing in this post-collapse world. RBS wouldn't even have needed to prompt these conversations because such debates were happening around screens, dinner tables and in front rooms up and down the country. People were engaged as the banks were bailed out, as executives got paid huge bonuses and as governments argued about savings, regulation and the future. RBS could also have engaged in this national debate, openly co-creating the future of banking with employees, customers, and potential customers demonstrating their commitment to changing previous poor behaviour and adopting a new, fundamentally more positive values set. What a missed opportunity for leadership.

why didn't RBS choose 'another way'?

The communications model needs to change and most corporations are way behind the curve and falling into the gap. This is most exposed in crisis, but is an ongoing issue, every day, which we have looked at here. In the next chapter, we move on to the key question: what makes for a high-trust organisation?

TAKE ACTION TO CO-CREATE WITH YOUR EMPLOYEES AND CUSTOMERS

Step 1: Are you caught in the gap?
• Examine the following questions.
   – What are the current issues that the brand is facing?

- What are the major reputation risks that you run?
- What is your communications model – top-down or side to side?
- Where do you run the greatest risk that you will be caught in the gap?
  - These will be those risks or situations where access to information affects the narrative and you are compromised in your response by the speed of your ability to change.
  - Look at your narrative (from previous chapters) and analyse it for potential risks and opportunities.
  - How can you start to develop plans to mitigate these risks (see Step 5)?

Step 2: Which of your customers really want to engage?
- Most of your customers just want to be left alone and will continue to reward you with their loyalty (or at least a part of it) – do you know which ones?
- Start an exercise to identify the most engaged customers and those who are temporarily engaged.
  - What are the drivers of their engagement?
  - How do you reflect these drivers in your marketing?

Step 3: From mass communications to mass interactions
- **Engagement**: Moving from a mass broadcast model to a mass interaction model
  - Where, how and why do those who are engaged want to interact with you?
  - How do you measure engagement?
  - What can you uniquely offer in the engagement?
- **Contention**: Using the power of contention to drive engagement.
  - What are the really important issues in your category or area of business?
  - What are people caring and talking about?
  - What is your opinion as a brand on these issues?
  - How can you contribute to these debates?

Step 4: Unleash the power of your people
- Create side-to-side communication
  - What do your current policies say?
  - How can you empower, trust and enable your people to have maximum impact through their communications?
  - What pilots can you set up to prove the case for side-to-side communications rather than top-down ones?
  - Are you falling into the trap of pretending your brand is social while gagging your employees who are?

Step 5: Scenario planning
- Create two scenarios – one positive and one negative – to test your response as an organisation and brand. Do you default to top-down communications?
  - **Negative** Imagine you have a major product quality issue that is picked up by the media and it begins to be magnified.
    - How would you respond today?
    - How could you use interactions to control and change the narrative?
  - **Positive** Imagine you have a major product launch that brings something truly new to the market.
    - Would you broadcast its positives today?
    - How could you interact your way to greatness?

Are you a high-trust organisation?

Do you trust your customer? How do you show it? Most businesses don't even trust themselves! Creating high-trust brands requires that your business is a high-trust culture, from its leadership down.

The 'dark triad' is the malevolent powers of Machiavellianism, psychopathy and narcissism. The traits covered by these are often ascribed to corporate power play: selfishness, impulsiveness, lack of empathy, playing politics, hubris and general disregard for others.

Machiavellian individuals are much more willing to stab people in the back than is the norm, as they plot and plan their social actions and reactions to get what they want. Narcissists exhibit self-aggrandisement, entertain fantasies of power and entitlement, are quick to take credit or defect and have a strong desire for social dominance. Psychopathic traits are the worst of the bunch, being chronically unstable, antisocial, thrill-seeking, aggressive and impulsive. Of the three traits, being a psychopath is the most overtly dangerous and the only one correlated with criminality.

These elements and the dark triad have been the subject of much study, including whether or not we have the ability to detect these traits in others and temper our trusting responses based on these hunches. Many of our decisions to trust are based on first impressions or very limited interactions and, therefore, must be rapid. Many of the prisoner's dilemma games that we discussed in other chapters involve limited or no social contact between participants. So, what signals do we use when choosing to trust or not?

Faces and the clues they contain about our background, attitude and personality are a rampant source of trust signals. Dr Alexander Todorov, an associate professor in psychology at Princeton University, together with colleagues (2005), completed a series of experiments that explored the power of faces to signal trust. They exposed the faces – only the faces – of candidates for political office in the USA to respondents who knew nothing else of these candidates, then asked the simple question, 'Who is more competent?'

Astonishingly, the results showed that, around 70 per cent of the time, the winning candidate was chosen just from looking at his or her face and, in some of the experiments, the results even mirrored the margin of victory. Even more astounding, though, is the length of time that people had to judge the face of the politician: only 100 milliseconds, one-tenth of a second. No time for analysis, looking deep into his or her eyes or engaging the conscious brain. The experimenters even found that the snap judgement was more reliable than when longer viewing times were given.

our snap decisions on who to trust are as important as the hundreds of millions spent on political advertising

The conclusion is that our snap decisions on who to trust are as important as the hundreds of millions spent on political advertising, hours spent on talk shows and interviews persuading us to vote. If you want to succeed in politics, get a trustworthy face.

These snap decisions come from a part of our brains called the *amygdala*, which has special functions in social cognition. Those with damaged amygdala consistently make inappropriate social decisions and rate an individual's trustworthiness opposite to how others rate it. What the amygdala processes is the clues from the faces we observe: attractiveness, self-resemblance, even facial geometry. It works super-fast and reacts strongly, especially in response to any perceived threat.

So, if we can detect who to trust, can we also detect who not to trust, and who might cause us harm? It's easy to imagine how an ability to avoid those that might stab us in the back could confer an evolutionary advantage.

In a fascinating experiment by researchers Dr David Gordon and Dr Steven Platek (2009), students were ranked on the 'dark triad' traits and their level of trustworthiness by answering a survey. Then photos were taken of them. Another group of students were then shown these photos while in an fMRI scanner, which has the ability to measure brain activity in real time. Over 10 minutes, they were shown the pictures a total of 168 times and their brain responses measured. The researchers were looking for how the brain – especially the amygdala – responded to those faces that were from individuals with higher survey scores on these dark triad traits.

When the Machiavellian and narcissistic faces were shown, those parts of our brains involved in making emotional and social decisions fired. There was no significant activation of the amygdala. When the faces were shown that were high in the negative traits related to psychopathy or the positive traits of trustworthiness, however, the amygdala was activated, significantly.

The study revealed that we have a deeper physiological response to both the potential threat of a psychopath and the potential benefit from someone we believe to be trustworthy. Seemingly, we have the ability, in one-tenth of a second, to decode who might do us harm or good.

we have the ability, in one-tenth of a second, to decode who might do us harm or good

With many of the corporate scandals of the past decade, there has been much discussion of corruption, ethics and morality in business. The popular myth of a typical corporate is that those at the top control the organisation for their personal aggrandisement, power and wealth, often at the expense of traditional virtues. It is easy to see the dark triad at work in WorldCom, Tyco, Enron and even some of the mistakes of the major banks.

In my experience, corporate life is much more humdrum, less political and Machiavellian than it is made out to be. The search for a high-trust organisational model is much more about effectiveness, long-term competitiveness and ensuring that the business can be trusted to do the right thing. This search is a profitable one on the journey to persuading the customer to trust your business and brand. If you can't get people in your organisation to trust each other, then how strong a chance do you have of delivering a trusted brand?

Trust is a two-way thing

Whether it is between mother or baby or tweeter and tweetee, trust is built through mutual relationships. Whether hugely deep or superficial, there is always some exchange that is enabled through trust. Yet, despite this, most businesses, especially the larger ones, have adopted a position and set of processes that manage for the downside risk, demonstrating they do not trust their customers. Corporations make decisions on customer experience that destroy trust, such as outsourcing key elements of the experience to third parties, often in far-flung parts of the world. Risk aversion causes businesses to constantly err on the side of caution and the more easily analysable. Try taking out a significant level of life assurance and, after the 50-page personal history and medical tests are over, you *might* be granted the insurance. Procurement departments, all in the name of risk mitigation, now insist on endless acronymed processes, disclosures and contractual clauses that cause a huge amount of increased cost and overhead – so much so that many small businesses often cannot afford to get involved.

most businesses ... manage for the downside risk, demonstrating they do not trust their customers

In financial services, risk models institutionalise and manage downside risk and, more often than not, take the approach that the customer is guilty until proven innocent. A person defaulting on a credit card can typically expect to receive multiple calls a day, increasing in their aggression, in order to recover the debt. Companies often operate a 'shock and awe' strategy, aggressive recovery activity happening as soon as a day after default to shock the customer back into line. They initiate the process first and ask questions later. The 'computer says no' approach pilloried by David Walliams and Matt Lucas in the comedy series *Little Britain* is so acerbic because it is so true. Too many companies and their employees operate through a set of rules, targets and measures and processes that have become a straitjacket, stifling trust.

Regulation often doesn't help either. Increasingly, there has been a defaulting to 'caveat emptor': as long as there is full disclosure, then almost anything is allowed. Prior to the financial collapse, regulators rarely made judgements on whether products were 'right' or 'wrong'. The emphasis is on the business to be transparent around every restriction or condition. A simple change in terms or conditions now often causes the reissuance of 100-page documents that customers rarely read and certainly don't build trust. It's not about making consumers empowered through awareness and understanding to make better choices but, rather, a process of ensuring that, should something go wrong, the business can say, 'but we told you so', even if this is buried on page 15, paragraph 6, subclause 12, line 19.

Does your business trust your customer?

Many businesses, brands, leaders and organisations obsess about whether or not people trust them. This has been a constant theme in newspapers and journals, especially over the past few years as trust has been perturbed. Rarely do brands or businesses ask themselves the associated questions, 'Do we trust our customers?' and 'How do we show it?' Trust is a two-way relationship so, if you only want the trust of your customer without being prepared to trust them in return, you reject the nature of what a trusting relationship really means.

rarely do brands or businesses ask themselves ... 'Do we trust our customers?' and 'How do we show it?'

Most businesses, I would argue, do not trust their customers and put most of their efforts into systematically managing distrust rather than systematically creating higher levels of trust (see Box 8.1). The irony is, more trust between the customer and brand would drive down the deleterious economics of fraud, for example, by creating a relationship that is valued and respected. This lack of trust impacts the attitude that staff have to customers. Instead of being a source of fair return, they are a source of downside risk to be managed and this attitude permeates service, too. The result is the creation of an increasingly adversarial relationship between customer and brand so that, both metaphorically and in reality, the customer is *more* likely to 'steal the towels' or game the system. If the business is going to stiff you, better to stiff them first.

The credit card market in the late 1990s and early 2000s is a good example. The market was profitable, loyal and relatively sleepy. The credit card was an extra product on top of your bank account or a Barclaycard, the only major brand. At the turn of the century profitability in the UK credit card industry was around £4 billion. Then the Internet and American players came in, such as Capital One and MBNA, launching aggressive price-based products focused on transferring balances between cards. Suddenly, the credit card was an acquisition product and it used all the tricks of marketing to win new customers. Millions switched and, as they did, they started to learn this product wasn't about loyalty, service and trust any more, it was about price, commodity and gaming the system. Within less than a decade, profitability fell to below £1 billion despite credit card usage peaking at 50 per cent of the market. This, in turn, caused a series of profit-boosting and trust-destroying practises, such as payment allocation, payment protection insurance and unasked-for increased credit limits that eroded any last vestiges of trust from the category.

Box 8.1 The top set the tone of trust
An interview with Srini Gopalan, Consumer Director Vodafone UK

The line crackles into life and a voice that I'm very familiar with greets me. I've finally tracked down Srini Gopalan, the ex-CEO of

---

Capital One in Europe, ex-CMO of T-Mobile in the UK and now Director of Vodafone's Consumer business in the UK, to talk about trust. Srini has worked for big global companies across India, the USA and the UK, taking increasingly senior management roles. By living through the credit crunch while leading a credit card company, through the merger of T-Mobile and Orange, through working for one of the UK's largest mobile operators, he has learned the hard way about building trust in teams and organisations. He is skilled in it and, I should know, since Srini was my boss for two years.

'A big part of creating a trusted business comes from within – the internal culture and how it affects whether people trust each other. Creating organisations where people trust each other both individually and collectively, where there is a sense of personal accountability and "in it together" is critical to success.'

I ask the obvious question, 'so how do you build a high trust organisation?'

Srini answers, 'A lot of it is to do with the tone that gets set at the top of the organisation. The direction that the CEO and top team take as to how they run their own relationships with each other is really important. This provides a set of signals about what they value and who they trust. It always surprises me that people think that, the higher you get in an organisation, the more it is about politics and back-stabbing. In my experience, the top team has more to lose from low trust than anyone else.'

I interrupt, keen to understand if there are any hallmarks or key behaviours of higher-trust organisations. 'I think assuming positive intent is a huge part of building trust. If you expect double-dealing you may well second-guess and destroy any chance of trust-building. You need to assume that people are fundamentally trustworthy because, in the vast majority of cases, they are.'

'Creating organisations where solving problems rather than scoring points is the focus of effort requires culture, values, behaviours and rewards. We tend to overestimate how difficult it is to change organisational culture and behaviour, whereas we tend to underestimate the power of incentives and rewards in driving that change. Most people want to work in a high-trust environment – it's fundamentally nicer – but even with the group who show a low-trust attitude, when the trust dynamic improves, even they change behaviour.'

Through our conversation, it is clear that Srini's attitude is organisations can change from low trust to higher and this is an important success-enabling journey. It starts, however, with yourself and your behaviour, moves through to the values, behaviour and processes of the business and all the way through to organisational design.

'It's not easy to create a deep culture of trust, but it is critical to sustainable success', says Srini as his final comment.

How do you show you trust?

Given that most businesses and their brands rarely think about whether *they* trust, it is unsurprising that they rarely show to their customers that they are trusted. Creating this is a powerful way to start the reciprocity between businesses and customers that reduces costs and increases loyalty.

Examples are so rare that, when they occur, they often enter customer service mythology. Nordstrom, an American shoes and clothing store, is the best example, with the now legendary 'tyre return' story. The story goes that a customer walked into a Nordstrom store in Alaska with two snow tyres and asked for a refund. The sales agent promptly refunded his money without a question, thanked him for his business and hoped he would shop there again.

Nordstrom doesn't and never has sold tyres. What this exemplifies is that Nordstrom's approach to service is to trust that the customer is right, even when he or she is provably wrong, and demonstrate that trust through action. Similarly, in the UK, the department store John Lewis is famous for its 'Never knowingly undersold', promise and generous attitude to replacing goods, always riding high in both customer satisfaction and trust surveys.

Trust, reputation and reciprocity are powerful forces for participants in a relationship and they modulate behaviour. A whole new economy is building up based on trust. eBay is the classic example, where the feedback and rating system provides transparency about reputation that encourages the trust to flow between participants. Kiva and Zopa are new peer-to-peer lending models that use reciprocity and reputation to ensure that money lent is paid back. Reportedly, Kiva, enjoys a 98.46 per cent repayment rate and Zopa 99.35 per cent. There is nothing really new about these models from a lending perspective. What they do is simply go back in time and employ the same approaches that our banks did many years ago, assessing people in a much more rounded fashion, understanding their reputation, asking about them to friends and neighbours, then using this to make a lending judgement, much like a bank manager might have done 50 years ago. What they demonstrate is that if you create the right environment, trust can power the business model, your organisation and the relationship between your brand and your customer. What creates high-trust organisations, though? See Box 8.2 and the rest of this chapter for some pointers.

Box 8.2 A lack of confidence in human decision making
An interview with Lord David Currie, chairman of the International Centre for Financial Regulation and former chairman of Ofcom

David Currie is a very thoughtful man who has spent much of his career thinking deeply about how the rules set through regulation create or hinder an environment where trust can either grow or wither. After seven years running OFCOM, one of the biggest regulatory bodies, David was often at the very centre of the debate

---

about how communications affect our society, people, businesses and brands.

'Trust is not expensive, but transparency is. To capture and harness trust makes business cheaper, but capturing trust is about openly demonstrating and evidencing trustworthiness that can be difficult and expensive, but it is a prerequisite in today's environment. One of the most important elements in any business and its system of governance is the decisions one makes over how to judge its impact and performance.' As David shares his deep experience of these issues he goes on, 'The effort required by transparency is huge but, by definition, you cannot be transparent about the future. Navigating the future requires human decision making and this is where we have often lacked confidence.'

We are sitting in David's inviting and interesting flat in Farringdon. When I ask about its location, which is unusual for a peer involved in the cut and thrust of Whitehall, he replies, tellingly, that escaping 'the Westminster bubble' is essential for both work and life.

David continues, 'This lack of confidence is significant. In financial services, maths became more important than judgement. Regulation, with all good intentions, moved away from rules and more into a principle-based approach, trying to sustainably guide human decisions rather than place rules around them.'

So, was principle-based regulation such as the UK Financial Services Authority's much-vaunted 'treating customers fairly' approach right, then I asked? 'Well yes and no,' David replied, 'the philosophy of ensuring that values and principles drive the behaviour in a business is right, but fundamentally values and principles can't be imposed, they come from within. Add to this the fact that prosecutions under TCF were small, it had no teeth and TCF was somewhat of a diversion from the main issues, which were in the wholesale markets.'

'So, is the state of corporate governance and regulation healthy?'
I ask. 'Governance in general works well, but success is all about
balance and the role of the shareholder is key – investors need to
be more vocal in making their views clear about current and future
direction. The process of people calling executives and businesses
to account through shareholding is powerful as the slow move back
to trust begins.'

Are you a high-trust organisation?

When Alan Fox died in 2002, one of the world's most original thinkers in industrial relations passed into history. Fox, from humble beginnings, rose to become one of the so-called, 'Oxford School of Industrial Relations'. This group was the most influential in the Donovan royal commission of 1965–1968 into trade unions and employers' associations in Britain.

Fox had seen many aspects of life, from the shop floor to the battlefield. He left school early and, at the age of 14, was working in a camera film factory when he wrote that workers were seen as, 'disposable units and of course we knew it.' He then fought in World War II, seeing how hierarchies in military forces worked, forming a belief that arbitrary authority was ineffective. He started his academic journey humbly with a work-related qualification in administration but, by 1950, he had graduated from Exeter College at the University of Oxford and took up a lectureship in 1963.

Together with colleagues, Alan Fox was part of a strand of thinking in industrial relations that saw the interests of employers and workers, via the trade unions, as equal in both social and moral status – an approach called *pluralism*. This way of thinking coloured much of the industrial agenda of the 1950s, 1960s and 1970s in the UK. Fox defined this as, 'a democratic state composed of sectional groups with divergent interests over which the government tries to maintain some kind of dynamic equilibrium.'

This was contrary to many of the prior forms of thinking that were more 'unitary', where managers 'know best' and always work in the best interests of the organisation. In the 1980s, a new form of unitary thinking arose, associated with deregulation, unfettered capitalism and free markets that the then Prime Minister Margaret Thatcher and President Ronald Regan pushed forward.

The lasting legacy of Alan Fox is his brave and radical journey away from these two poles of pluralism and unitarism. In the early 1970s, Fox stood against what he saw as the ideological nature of pluralism. In his mind, this ideology stood in the way of progress because it served to maintain an unequal relationship between hired labour and capital and, therefore, was a way of simply reinforcing the status quo. In his later works, Fox describes a way of creating organisations that is fundamentally one based on morality, values, mutual interdependency, problem solving and positive intent. No longer a pluralist 'them versus us' or a unitary 'the manager is always right', but a more complex and fundamentally more social organism. See Box 8.3 for some insight into the role of trust in organisations.

Box 8.3 The trust power of leadership

● Leadership's role in creating high-trust organisations cannot be underestimated. Srini Gopalan, Director of Vodafone's consumer business in the UK, said in my interview with him, 'trust in organisations is signalled and comes from the top. That is where people look for direction about their behaviour. If they see people undermining and knifing each other in the back, then this will be replicated across the organisation.'

● Calling on his experience at T-Mobile in the UK – an organisation going through significant changes while he was there – he said, 'These changes can be relatively quick. There is always opportunity to signal change by making examples of specific people, situations or behaviours. These examples become powerful agents of change.'

- The majority of people working in businesses in the UK trust both their line manager and their CEO. This trust comes under increasing pressure as recessions bite and organisations change in size. In a study by the Institute of Leadership and Management, CEOs achieved an indexed score of 72 in organisations with fewer than 10 employees, which fell to 56 for those running organisations larger than a 1000. The impact of the recession, closing factories or offices, involuntary redundancies, voluntary redundancies, introduction of flexible working/reduced hours, departmental restructuring, recruitment freezes and tighter controls on spending, all negatively affected trust. Unsurprisingly, when these effects were experienced, trust in CEOs moved from 68 to 51 and line managers from 72 to 63. These scores are based on an index of six dimensions of trust, which, in order of importance, are integrity, ability, fairness, consistency, openness and understanding.

- The relationships between people and their leaders are incredibly important to the health of an organisation – they create the backbone of trust. Closely monitoring these relationships, using leaderships to demonstrate desired behaviours and moulding the narrative are important in creating a high-trust organisation.

Ideas for creating a high-trust organisation

In his classic 1974 book, *Beyond Contract: Work, power and industrial relations*, Fox presents a framework for creating a high-trust organisation that is still powerful today. He outlines five elements:

- aligning employees and managers around company goals and values
- changing the control system towards emphasising employees' own self-control

- developing coordination by mutual adjustment
- implementing a learning culture
- implementing a problem-solving approach to conflict resolution.

Fox's analysis came from UK industry in the 1970s and he identified the powerful movement away from what he termed 'high-dependency work', characterised by manual and often repetitive operations such as in a factory, to 'low-dependency work', which could be much more self-directed, much more the 'knowledge' work of today.

Luckily, much of the work in large organisations over the past 20 years has focused on trying to create these trust-based systems. We have discussed in previous chapters the weaknesses in many of the mission, vision and values statements, but at least they are an attempt to align people with a common purpose.

The next steps towards higher-trust organisations

Comparative studies of organisations that are high-trust and low-trust examine in detail the employee and leadership behaviours that foster trust. The work of Frédérique Six, together with Arndt Sorge, Douglas Creed and Raymond Miles, builds from Alan Fox's framework to drive us towards what high-trust organisations do.

trust in organisations needs to flow from relationships where showing care for others is supported, valued and embedded

Six and Sorge identified that trust in organisations needs to flow from relationships where showing care for others is supported, valued and embedded within principles shared throughout the business. Creed and Miles created a powerful new management philosophy called the *human investment philosophy*. The fundamental basis of this is the recognition that people *want* to contribute and are both trustworthy and anxious to be trusting in their relationships.

If your organisation truly wants to create trust, then it must be more than just window-dressing through marketing or communications – there needs to be a fundamental change in order to achieve trustworthiness and regain people's trust. We have explored the concept of brands as a form of social capital and, next, I'd like to extend this further into how organisational social capital can be cultivated to give a better chance of winning in the market.

Is your business rich in social capital?

Organisations that are high in trust are rich in social capital. They have a mythology, a narrative, strong leadership stories past and present, a way of doing things and a heart, head and soul. They are creative, positive places that attempt to achieve balance. From the studies of high-trust organisations they exhibit the following behaviours (see Figure 8.1).

organisations that are high in trust are rich in social capital

- **Trust-based control** Most control systems in businesses are hierarchical and mitigate risk rather than empower local decision making through trust. If the insights of Crèed and Miles are right, and I believe they are, then people *are* trustworthy and *want* to trust and be trusted. This is a powerful motivator. Consistently, those firms that, for example, move away from rule books and risk aversion to trusting frontline customer service agents to give refunds, waive policies and use their discretion with the customer achieve much higher satisfaction levels.

- **Comfortable with vulnerability** Businesses, especially male-dominated corporations, need to become comfortable with vulnerability. For example, admitting mistakes at all, and not even authentically, is still uncommon. Whether that is Toyota and its recall, BP in the Mexican Gulf or even Steve Jobs and the iPhone

Figure 8.1 Key elements that aid in the creation of a high-trust organisation, rich in social capital

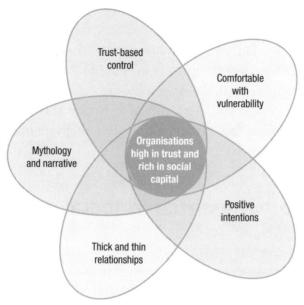

4, really 'fessing up and making yourself vulnerable is a very rare virtue. Ask Hilary Clinton whether or not shedding a tear and being vulnerable, if only for the briefest of moments, actively creates trust and loyalty.

● **Positive intentions** There are generally lots of 'What?' and 'How?' questions in businesses, but fewer about 'Why?' ones about the business choosing a particular course of action. Motivations, though, are powerful for customers in establishing trust and they are powerful *within* the organisation, too.

● **Thick and thin relationships** Much of the social capital within firms resides in the relationships between people. Those companies with a rich heritage, such as Procter & Gamble, gain huge value from this. In the 1990s when I joined the firm, I was packed off for a global orientation programme in Cincinnati, with participants from all over the world. It was a powerful experience on many levels. Investing in global orientation, internal research symposia, knowledge-sharing, network creation, early investment in intranet infrastructure and, most famously, the strict adherence to 'promoting from within' means many relationships are cultivated that have become the social capital base of the firm.

● **Mythology and narrative** The internal narrative and mythology of a business is just as important as the external, yet it receives much less attention. All the best brands and businesses have a powerful internal mythology and storyline that ebbs and flows across time. From Hewlett & Packard to Procter & Gamble to Page & Brin, all the great brands have rich stories that bound and bind their values, their cultures and their behaviours. The constant consolidation in banking in the 1990s led to an almost complete lack of values, mythology and coherent narrative in many banking groups and this is at least partially to blame for their collapse. Those that survived relatively unscathed, such as HSBC, JP Morgan and Deutsche Bank, all enjoy a very strong sense of internal culture and rich narrative history.

These elements, in combination with the other facets of organisational dynamics and change, can create the high-trust organisations, rich in social capital, that can power the brands needed to repair the standing of business in the twenty-first century.

High-trust organisations will create connections around ideas and problems that matter – not just commercially but also in the world and to our communities. This will be the landscape of brand leadership in the future as businesses find more balanced ways to demonstrate value. We explore this in the next chapter.

TAKE ACTION TO CREATE A HIGH-TRUST ORGANISATION

Step 1: Do you trust your customer?
- How do you assess risk in your business?
  - Have you institutionalised a position of low trust in your customer?
  - Are there any areas where you actively *do* trust your customer?

- Can you create more of these areas?
  - How can you leverage the power of trust to replace institutionalised distrust? Can you test this approach?
- How do you signal that you trust or distrust your customer?
  - What are the key elements of your customer experience? Do they engender trust or distrust?
  - Are there any areas where you could actively signal that you trust your customer?
  - Can you create or identify opportunities to demonstrate that you trust, such as in returns or fee policies?

Step 2: Are you a high-trust organisation?
- Re-examine your thoughts from Chapter 1.
  - How well aligned are people in your organisation with the company's goals and values?
  - Does your organisation run through self-control or imposed control?
  - Does your organisation operate through mutual readjustment?
  - Do you have a learning culture?
  - Do you resolve conflict through politics or problem solving?
- What are the signals and stories that come from the leadership of the organisation? Are they trust-building or destroying?

Step 3: Creating a high-trust organisation
- Creating systems of trust-based control: Can you find opportunities to move from command and control to self-control and trust? Can you experiment?
- Are you comfortable with vulnerability? How can you celebrate mistakes and learn from them? Could you run 'mistake' sessions where you identify the learning opportunities? When was the last time you said sorry for something you've done at work?
- Creating an environment of positive intentions. Is your organisation or team operating on the assumption of positive intent? How can you create opportunities to move towards the positive intentions?

What assumptions do you carry around when you interact with others?

- Thick and thin relationships. Does your organisation intentionally create opportunities for relationships to grow? Do you share knowledge and experiences across teams?
- Mythology and narrative. What is your internal narrative? What are the things that your organisation holds true and how does this relate to the external narrative? Do they align with each other or are they dissonant? How can you help create new elements of the narrative to encourage an environment of trust

Living-room leadership

'Living-room leadership' is the spark that lights the way to a re-establishment of trust in business. Brands committing to a mission that uses their resources to help solve serious issues deserve to win trust.

World War II created a schism in trust that reverberated across the world and dictated the landscape until the end of the Cold War. Swarthmore psychologist and author of *The Paradox of Choice* Barry Schwartz (2005) says, 'the secret to happiness is ... low expectations.' World War II painfully and tragically reset expectations and set them low.

The brightness of the ideals and innovation that eventually came in the 1950s emerged from the darkness of a previous decade where 70 million people perished. The Welfare State in Britain, the realignment of interests in Europe and Asia, industrial and domestic innovation in the USA, were great achievements, giving the world a fundamentally more positive and stable outlook. Standards of living improved in an economy powered by consumption and it felt good. There was even the visceral comparison with communism to show just how well capitalism was doing. The baby boomer generation and its children grew up in a world of seemingly endless resources and possibilities.

Despite the inevitable booms and busts, the industrial unrest of the 1970s and the individualism of the 1980s, these post-war decades were times when the global order seemed set and the stable path to prosperity and growth was never-ending. Trust and hope for the future was high. Of course there were incidents of low trust, impeached presidents, global crises, wars, business collapses, but, fundamentally, the system didn't need to be questioned.

The world is different now. We live in a system and world that looks and *feels* unsure of itself and this is unsettling. The 'matrix' that we created

the 'matrix' that we created to support a high-growth, high-consumption economic model is crumbling

to support a high-growth, high-consumption economic model is crumbling. The twenty-first century has started with more questions than answers.

The twentieth century saw America becoming the global superpower, with economic and cultural dominance. We now look to the South and East, with their very different cultural and economic models. These fast-growing economies see the direct benefits of employment, increasing quality, prosperity coming from the rise of commerce, while, in the West, most people don't remember why we need to encourage business and why we create markets to support these enterprises.

Business in the West is seen as for the scoundrels, the fat cats, those looking to feather their own nests. Rather than being a source of equality and rising standards of living for all, business is now seen as a source of inequality. Bankers, as the top 'predators' in this system, blindly and conspicuously continue to dole out millions to their staff in bonuses, which reinforces this perception.

Business has become unbalanced. Stakeholders have been forgotten in deference to the almighty shareholder. Nothing has been more important for the leadership of businesses over the past 30 years than an almost maniacal focus on the markets and their short-term demands. These demands and those of institutional or short-term shareholders, such as hedge funds, allow great businesses rich in social capital and trust to be sold to the highest bidder. Britain with its commitment to free markets without trade restrictions, now has virtually none of the brands

Britain ... now has virtually none of the brands or businesses that made it great

or businesses that made it great. Cadbury sold to Kraft, Wedgwood in the hands of private equity firm KPS Capital Partners of New York or Tomkins, the global engineering and manufacturing company founded in 1925 now owned by Onex, the Canadian private equity firm, are just a few examples. Stakeholders, past, present and future, are seen as a distraction. This thinking leads to unbalanced and fundamentally unsustainable outcomes.

All this is happening in a changing world context. 'It's a small world' has never seemed so true. We are used to hearing this in terms of communication, culture or travel, but we are now realising that, with a population of 7 billion, set to rise to 9 to 10 billion by 2050, our planet is just too small if we continue on the path we are on. Environmental change and resource depletion are the direct result of our insatiable consumption. We are using our world up and this will have consequences. Increasingly for consumers, this leaves a bad taste in the mouth with every purchase.

If all this weren't enough to contend with, we have seemingly conspired to underline, italicise and highlight the lack of sustainability in our economy with a financial and economic collapse the like of which hasn't been seen since the Great Depression. The past few decades of increasing financial innovation have fuelled and been fuelled by our increasing acceptance of debt.

Debt rests on trust: the trust that the money will be paid back. We have seen this simple truth play out over the past few years. Despite all the maths, the models, the cleverest brains in the world, all the resources, when the money isn't paid back, the foundation of trust is shown to be not on rock but sand.

The great fallacy we have lived through has been that we could borrow without *ever* paying back. Both individually and nationally we trusted that rising house prices, economic growth, full employment, financial cleverness, inflation, currency movements, the power of capitalism, something would save the day, we could feast forever.

The party is over and now we have to start to repay and rebuild trust.

Leaders: apply within

What we need now, desperately, is leadership. Not just Obama-style big band, big concept leadership, but down-to-earth everyday leadership that we can interact with, discuss with others and be moved by. The sort of living-room leadership that brands and business can exert. Consumerism has been aided by the ability of businesses and brands to change what we value and our behaviour. It is now time for businesses and their brands to step up to the plate, recognise their role in social capital construction and get on a mission. This is the spark that will light the way to a re-emergence of business and commerce as a direct force for the common good.

The future landscape of brand leadership will be played out through businesses that understand and get comfortable with this role and recognise that, through the fundamental action of their business model, the interactions they have with their stakeholders and the resources at their disposal, they can make *the* key difference.

social missions in today's context need to stem from the collective will of the business to catalyse actions ... to get stuff done

Apart from anything else, I believe this is the right thing to do, but, more than this, in our transparent world, where intentions and actions are available to view for anyone with an Internet connection, these social missions have the ability to command greater trust and loyalty from people and become a source of competitive advantage.

Businesses playing a conspicuous role in the common good of society is nothing new. However, the context is fundamentally different, changing expectations and opportunities. As we have noted, businesses are no longer seen as good *per se*, but there is something broader, more challenging going on. Great, common good businesses of the past – the Cadburys, the Wedgwoods – all operated from a paternalistic perspective. We now have a new, more democratic society, the balance of power has shifted and expectations have changed. So, social missions in today's context need to stem from the collective will of the business to catalyse actions through their resources, their connections, their ability to motivate and inspire and their ability to get stuff done.

Living-room leadership is the process of building social influence and collective action in order to effect a change towards a specific goal. Brands have been leading in the living-room for generations, but often the social effects of their actions and messages have been an unconscious byproduct of winning in the market. This must no longer be the case. Business models need to be adapted so that a virtuous circle is created where, the more a customer buys the product or service, the more good is done and the greater the contribution to social capital.

This is at the very heart of our core question – why should anyone buy from you? Nowadays, when product quality is so high, innovation so fleeting, marketing games less and less effective and loyalty so low, the real answer to this question is because you are a fundamentally *better* company. Not, or at least not only, because you are better at your core business, but better because of your contributions to the common good. In *The Next Evolution of Marketing* by Bob Gilbreath, a study by Duke University showed that 87 per cent of consumers will switch from one brand to another based on an association with a good cause. People trust people and companies that do good.

87 per cent of consumers will switch from one brand to another based on an association with a good cause

Big problems, big opportunities, big connections

The problems that we are facing as a world, especially in Western societies, are huge and causing needs to change – consumers are worried and confused. This is a tremendous landscape in which to create powerful new connections with people. The reworking and reformulation of products and services so that they are less polluting, healthier and less damaging will increasingly be seen as basic expectations. What leadership brands do to differentiate and create powerful connections will be to compete through their ideals, their aspirations to make a difference and the way they employ their resources to achieve these aims.

Those brands that prosper in this new environment will adopt social roles that create connections between the needs and concerns of their customers, balance their impact on stakeholders and fundamentally link to their core purpose, going way beyond the current view of 'corporate social responsibility' (CSR) or cause-related marketing

CSR is not an effective response to the concerns around a lack of balance in corporate behaviour. The model of CSR is almost unchanged in principle from the patronage of artists and musicians by Florentine merchants in the fifteenth century who used a small portion of their profit, often from unscrupulous activity, to curry favour. CSR is often still a veneer over the business' main activities. Donations to art collections, school sponsorships, bursaries, promoting staff time and skills, donations to the ballet or environmental projects can't make up for a core business that creates, either consciously or unconsciously, malign outcomes for any stakeholder. Cause-related marketing can be even worse, seeking to gain attention for a brand by superficially picking up an issue and buying

CSR is often still a veneer over the business' main activities the right to talk about it. This is rarely done out of a true desire to make a difference but, rather, a desire to use the cause to sell more product. The Internet and radical transparency today help to expose when these activities are window-dressing rather than a serious attempt to intentionally intervene and make a serious contribution.

What customers want to know in order to trust is where you are coming from and what drives you to do what you do. Most people accept that businesses need to make a fair return for giving a benefit but, today, this is too hollow a basis for asking for their trust. People, more and more, expect that this return is not made at the expense of the environment, social capital or exploitation. They want to see businesses that take their stakeholder responsibilities seriously and aspire to play for higher goals. Those brands that create a culture of delivery around a social mission will create powerful reasons why customers should engage.

Pampers, for example – one of the most trusted brands in the world – is a major P&G success story. They managed to move a disparate and disjointed global brand that focused almost solely on product benefits into a unique and powerful connection with mothers by understanding the power of mission. Pampers understood that they needed to be idealistic, not just from a product performance perspective but also from the viewpoint of mums everywhere. They created a brand ecosystem that included mothers, their children, children's fathers and grandparents and key partners to ensure that mothers and babies get the advice and support they need. A partnership with UNICEF includes the aim to rid the world of newborn and maternal tetanus by 2012. Another with the Royal College of Midwives in the UK means Pampers produces a free guide to the first 12 weeks of being a mum. With the National Childbirth Trust, they provide antenatal packs and DVDs. Clearly, Pampers also still have challenges, as the need for environmental performance and product sustainability become ever greater. Pampers have made relatively small changes to the product to date, but are working on technologies that will be biodegradable in the future.

The power of ideals, and their active demonstration of your intentions, in building trust are not to be doubted. Brands and the marketers that run them have the opportunity to use the significant resources at their disposal to effect very great change in our world through the adoption of the right mission. No corporate budget is more open and flexible than the marketing budget and no department more attuned to the needs of humanity (see Box 9.1).

Box 9.1 The future of marketing
An interview with Tom Farrand, founder of Pipeline (www.pipelineproject.co)

Tom Farrand, founder of Pipeline, is a brand thinker, the like of which I've never encountered before. Part scientist, part consultant, part creative, Tom thinks through brands and their impact on the world with a huge brain and a bigger heart. His consultancy Pipeline takes on very few projects, even though it is in huge demand, choosing to, as he puts it, 'Only work with people that are open to exploring new ways to tackle the challenge of business sustainability.'

'People are starting to take into account different factors and information when making their decisions. Their prioritisation of what is important is changing. It's sometimes driven by sustainability issues, but it often runs deeper than that, to questions about their wellbeing, their families and the communities they live and work in,' Tom is breaking down the changing landscape of trust as he sees it.

'People are learning to make much more conscious decisions about who they want to do business with and why. If we go back to basics – marketing at its core is about finding out what people want and responding to those needs. Marketing needs to reframe the definition of need. To dig deeper, get out from behind the glass, and explore the real issues in peoples' lives – their real human needs not manufactured wants and their hopes and fears for the future.'

We discuss the role of marketing in the corporation. 'Marketing is uniquely placed to marry up the left and right brains of a business. You have all the skill sets and talents to really understand what people want and combine this with measurement and systems which can change behaviour.'

'When you hear a company say, for example, "We have an engineering, or product or sales-driven culture," what this really means is that they are bad at being human – bad at listening and empathising and making emotional decisions. Marketing is one of the few places in an organisation where you can get that balanced view,' says Tom as we try to define what the future of marketing could look like.

'People's changing priorities as both citizens and consumers, and the balancing role for marketing in business creates so many opportunities to engage on the important issues that are behind what is fundamentally going on in many categories. Businesses that manage to create and communicate their sustainable value will be the winners of the future.' Tom is starting to develop a theme here.

'How do you see this playing out?' I ask.

'Brands and businesses need to recognise and embrace the social roles that they play in peoples' lives and the impact that they have on broader society. A good way to think about business is the impact it will have on the future of the *planet* and a good way to think about marketing is the impact it will have on people's minds and behaviour to create that future.'

I ask, 'Are brands really starting to get this?' 'The smartest companies like Nike, GE, Nestlé, Unilever, Patagonia and Puma are leading the way. They've spotted an opportunity to create shared value, innovate with purpose and build a more sustainable future. They've recognised that people will demand higher standards and confer loyalty on those companies that can do the fundamental basis of marketing well but in a fundamentally new context.'

Mission possible

How do we formulate what our mission and ideals should be? There are four key elements that need to come together in order to adopt a social mission that will powerfully build trust and can exemplify your brand's living-room leadership (see Figure 9.1). You will need to consider each of

Figure 9.1 The four key elements of a powerful, trust-building mission

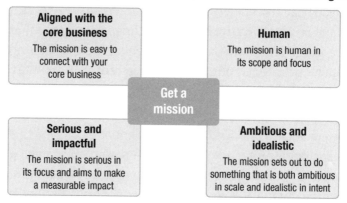

these when you start to assess the sparks that you have already in your business and brand.

ALIGNED WITH THE CORE BUSINESS

Many businesses and brands are side-tracked by things that are *not* aligned with the core business. This is often in the name of awareness-building or even a vanity project by the business and its leadership. The best examples of these misaligned activities are in the arts and sporting arenas. Not *all* these activities are misaligned per se, especially if there is a deep passion within the employees for these activities, but, often, they are superficial and done at the expense of other more pressing, more business-aligned priorities.

social brand missions that work the best are those which are aligned deeply with the core business

Social brand missions that work the best are those which are aligned deeply with the core business. Unsurprisingly, this is because they are more authentic, engaging and credible. The engagement comes from the passion that the brand has for its core business and related social missions; credibility comes from its unique point of view.

The Body Shop, most powerfully in its early days under the leadership of Anita Roddick, was a business powered by an idealistic vision to create a beauty company that could be sustainable and ethical. This propelled it into the minds and hearts of customers and often on to the front page. The campaigning position of the brand was maintained and supported strongly by both the product and sourcing decisions that the business made. The Body Shop was both engaging and credible on the issues of sustainability and beauty to which it committed.

Nike brilliantly inspire millions around the world to get up and stay active. Their 'Human Race' activities get thousands running in cities the world over. They are open, they are inclusive and they get many of those who haven't run to start. Experiencing one of these events is to live Nike's mission of 'bringing inspiration and innovation to every athlete in the world.' Nike often don't achieve a sustainable balance in their activities but, because their mission is clear, they have a much greater chance of attaining trust.

HUMAN

The social imperatives that underlie the missions of brands and businesses should be human in their scope and focus. What I mean by this is that the efforts should be focused on important human needs for the well-being of individuals, communities or society. The business model on which the brand is based should create socially beneficial outcomes.

The cooperative movement works to ensure that, as it succeeds in its core businesses, contributions are fairly distributed back to the supply chain. Even a hugely commercial brand such as Coca-Cola has understood over the years the power of creating a mission around a human emotion – happiness. This has worked to propel the brand forwards, aligning with its idealistic, new world, American heritage and a product that is all about a moment of delight. Coke has used this to connect powerfully with its customers and demonstrate why they should buy. Clearly, Coca-Cola also has to ensure the sustainability of their mission to spread happiness to all stakeholders past, present and future.

AMBITIOUS AND IDEALISTIC

Missions should be ambitious and idealistic. Too many brands and businesses aim low or seek to connect on ground that just isn't big enough to command attention. If you are going to adopt a social mission for your business, then why not make it ambitious in its scope? This doesn't mean that you can't also be practical and action-oriented.

When the Innocent brand puts packets of seeds on their bottles or little woolly hats at Christmas or badges to promote World Peace Day, they do this because of their ambition as a brand to make a difference. They are idealistic in the causes they partner with and they work best when they are deeply aligned with the core business. Their support for the honey bee is an example of where their support is inextricably linked to their main raw material and also their brand attitude.

When Pepsi ditched their Superbowl advertising to launch the $20m Refresh Project, they were putting their ideals ahead of the traditional approach to attention-grabbing media. Pepsi gained a huge amount of engagement from people because they were ambitious in the sums being invested and the concept of moving advertising money away from traditional media into socially impactful grants in education, health, environmental and cultural projects.

SERIOUS AND IMPACTFUL

The trouble with too much brand marketing is that it seeks to connect with people on frivolous and inconsequential subjects. This isn't a problem in and of itself – the trouble is that it generally sucks up so much investment money it becomes a *waste* of money, even if it *does* produce a nominal return.

when you get on a mission as a business or a brand, it should be with serious intent to have a major impact

When you get on a mission as a business or a brand, it should be with serious intent to have a major impact. This doesn't have to be on a global or national level. There are so many local issues that can form the basis of significant engagements with people that this is often a very fruitful area. I am consistently amazed that more brands don't seek to engage with people on a local basis.

Patagonia is a brand that has decided to seriously and impactfully adopt mission at the centre of its business. The mission statement of this company is, 'Build the best product, cause no unnecessary harm, use business to inspire, and implement solutions to the environmental crisis.' Patagonia use their marketing to get their customers involved, with them, in fighting for good environmental outcomes. All their materials celebrate the beauty of nature and how fragile it is. This company has integrated the process of meeting its mission into everything it does, from donations of more than $25 million to having a person in each meeting who plays the role of representing the views of future generations. Patagonia is having a serious impact with its form of living-room leadership.

Nestlé have integrated human and societal impacts into the way that they do business. Their 'Creating shared value' approach integrates compliance and sustainability with a belief 'that in order to create long-term value for shareholders, we have to create value for society.' This goes beyond the traditional approach to CSR. Nestlé applies their resources, in terms of money and talent, to tackling significant issues for their global communities, specifically in nutrition, water and rural development. This will run, according to the company, to a total investment of nearly a billion dollars over the next decade.

Start at the beginning

This journey to get a mission can seem daunting. Where do you start and how do you win over the organisation or your boss? The most important thing to remember is that adopting a mission is a good thing to do and a noble cause. It might not be easy, but is it ever

adopting a mission ... might not be easy, but is it ever worthwhile

worthwhile – and it might even help you answer the question of 'What is my job for?'

The first focus should be on finding a mission that can be driven by your business model and fits with your brand. These discussions can either happen at the level of people around the business or the people leading the business or even better, both. The key is to find something that meets the criteria. Get clear on what the business needs the brand to do and then get clear on what society needs the brand to do.

The next thing to realise is that, even if you are in a relatively small company, your marketing budget will be a significant amount of money. I am constantly frustrated by hearing marketers, especially in the past few years, bemoan the 'lack of budget' or cuts in their budgets when they are still spending millions. Even the 'just' thousands of an advertising campaign could have a significant effect if spent elsewhere. It is worth bearing in mind that the average primary school in the UK runs on much less than £1 million per annum and a course of treatment for a cancer patient can cost less than £10,000.

There is always room to try and invest in some form of activity that can drive progress against your mission. The thing is to start and build. There will always be opportunities to use your activity in internal or external communications and they don't need to be in the form of big bang advertising, but engaging and credible stories that inspire and prove your intentions are in the right place.

By getting a mission, you fast track to a seam of trust-building that is powerful and, if you get it right, authentic. The future of trust will be a radical one. There are powerful forces at work in the environment, in our economies, in our minds and in our hearts. The businesses that will thrive will need to positively embrace these changes and see them as opportunities, not threats. That is the focus of the final chapter.

TAKE ACTION TO DISCOVER YOUR MISSION

Step 1: What is the impact of your business?
- Stakeholder analysis.
  - What is the impact of your business and brand on each of your stakeholders?
    - Examine customers, shareholders, employees, suppliers, community and society at large.
    - Look at all you do – from product through to production through to marketing messages
    - Look at it from the perspectives of the past, present and future.
- Current prioritisation and processes.
  - How do your business and brand currently prioritise their impact? Look at the outcomes/objectives set – which stakeholders do they pay more attention to?
  - In your planning and objective-setting processes, how do the needs of the different stakeholders get prioritised?
- From your analysis, do you have a true social mission that you are committed as an organisation or brand to deliver or are you just paying lip-service to it?

Step 2: What does society need from your brand?
- What is your brand for?
- What is your job for? Does your answer satisfy you?
- What does society need from your brand?
- What issues in society are important to your brand and affect it directly?
- What is your brand's opinion and impact on its issues?

Step 3: Finding your mission
- From your analysis in step 2, create a matrix of issues that affect your brand and score them high/medium/low on the following four elements of building a trusted brand mission.

- **Aligned with the core business** How can the issue be impacted by your business model and brand? Does your brand have or could have a relevant point of view or expertise on the issue?
- **Human** What are the human impacts of the issues? How can your brand and business model seek to impact these human aspects?
- **Serious and impactful** Would any attempts by your brand to engage in these issues be serious with a high chance of making a measurable positive impact?
- **Ambitious and idealistic** Would any mission be ambitious in its scope and idealistic in its pursuit? How could you focus your efforts to make a real difference?

Step 4: Unleashing your mission
- Create a plan to gain alignment/clarification on the social role for your brand.
- Look at all current activities from CSR to external communications to marketing, to see where overlaps and opportunities lie.
- Make a start – if necessary – start small and test.

The future of trust

There is a radical future out there ready to be taken. Big change is on the horizon and how we respond to those changes will determine whether we stick a plaster over the cracks or sustainably solve the question of trust in our businesses and brands.

'Is it wrong to make a profit?' I was asked quietly by the priest sitting opposite me. 'Well, no,' I replied, 'but surely it depends on how you make it, and for what end.'

This interview seemed to be revealing something different from the others that I'd conducted for this book – a deeper, more personally challenging exploration of morality and the role of business.

Fr Jack Maloney SJ, an 80-year-old Jesuit priest seemed to be less interested in telling me what *he* thought about trust and more interested in challenging me about *my* judgements – a rather Jesuitical trait. Fr Jack cocked his head slightly, 'So, by that analysis, you might say there is good and bad profit? But who defines what is good and bad?'

'In our current version of capitalism, I suppose it's the shareholder – isn't it?' I struggled. 'But are they the only people who should matter?' Fr Jack gently asked.

'No, there are other important stakeholders as well as shareholders: customers, employees, management, government, regulators, society at large, the environment – they all matter, don't they?' I suggested.

Fr Jack closed his eyes momentarily, smiled and turned to me: 'Our economic system is a complex balance, and businesses have a moral responsibility to create outcomes that balance the needs of all different stakeholders. The judgement of good or bad profit must be the outcome of this interrelated system of checks and balances between stakeholders – everyone has rights *and* responsibilities. Trust is the glue that binds stakeholders together in a common purpose; it's through balance that trust is created or destroyed.'

We discussed what had gone wrong with the economy over the past few years and the effects it was having on people around the world. We wondered together about how to put it right. We were coming to the end of our time together and Fr Jack asked me one last unassuming question: 'The jobs that you've done, what were they for?'

the jobs that you've done, what were they for?

A few minutes later, Fr Jack shook my hand and wished me the best of luck with my exploration of trust in business. I walked into the pretty gardens that surround the Mount Street church in London's Mayfair and sat. An hour later, I was still pondering Fr Jack's last question: what *had* my career – all those hours and nights away from home – been *for*?

Bankers are evil, aren't they?

I've spent much of the last ten years of my career working for banks, either as a consultant or employee, and I've been haunted by the financial collapse. I still have many friends who work in the financial services industry. The average man or woman on the street, especially at the moment, would class these friends as the type of people to be vilified and hated. They might say I'm in the same boat.

I don't think, though, that, when I worked for a bank, I was fundamentally very different from who I am now and I don't think my friends, still working for Deutsche Bank or Royal Bank of Scotland or any other financial institution, are any worse than the rest of us. Yet, certainly, when I left the investment banking world, it was because I looked around at people ten years older than me and I knew that I didn't want to be like them. The atmosphere seemed compromised, somehow, by the single-minded pursuit of money and, for me at least, it didn't sit right.

In a thought-provoking book, *Virtue Reborn*, the Anglican Bishop Tom Wright's (2010) diagnosis is, 'in our late-modern or post-modern world that to maximise your own (or your firm's) bank balance has, for many, become the deepest level of truth they can imagine.' This is just so terribly bleak and depressing, but I recognise it. Many of us are trapped in the complex system of expectations, targets, endless performance management that holds our feet to the fire of the material, the profitable, the commercial, in service of the shareholder above all else, including, in many cases, our families, our world, our communities and our own dignity. This system supports our unsustainable consumption-based economy and it needs to change.

Envisaging change for this system is hard and changing it will be even harder, but it needs to be done. 'The only thing necessary for the triumph of evil is for good men to do nothing' is the key thought that we must all hold on to as we go through this journey to something different and hopefully better. The easier course is to reject the need for change, either because it's too hard to get your head around or too easy just to trust that our direction of travel is OK and, therefore, just keep going. I urge you, however, to answer Fr Jack's question.

'What is your job for?'

Business and its brands are in the front line of our consumption economy. This question is especially vexing for marketers, given their role in creating the drive for consumption. I was speaking at a conference about sustainability in 2009, representing the role that business and the marketing it creates can play in moving us to a better and more sustainable system. A young woman raised her hand and asked me, 'Surely the best thing marketers can do for the planet is just give up and go home?' There are many who would agree with her. Many people think that the world would be a better place without the marketers, the bankers and the fat cats.

The basis for this perspective comes from a position of exclusivity, that the best way to drive the changes we surely need to make is to identify the 'them' who need to be stopped and the 'us' who can save the world. You pick a team and go from there, 100 per cent committed to defeating or defending the status quo. I believe that the next few decades, as we approach 9 to 10 billion people on the face of our planet, will bring profound change to the world and business. We will have to give up on much of what we believe to be true and start reformulating a new way for all of us to thrive. The alternative is conflict, intense competition for scarce resources and increasingly unhealthy and disjointed societies consuming themselves as they consume the world.

I hope we still have time so that this conflict can be avoided. Many people I respect in the sustainability movement do not agree, though. They believe that the system is too entrenched and there needs to be much more radical change imposed. I argue from a position of inclusion – that everyone should be a change agent in his or her own way, not just at home but also at work. Changing the system, regaining trust by adopting social roles for brands and businesses, is something that every person working in business, whether CEO or contract cleaner, can do something about. I recognise that many see marketers as some of the worst offenders of all – changing people's hearts and minds to crave the short term and consumerist – but I hope I have explored in some small way in these pages, the power of communication and ideas flowing from the use of marketing's skills and knowledge can be a powerful catalyst for change and the rehumanisation of business. This will fundamentally create the trusted brands and businesses of the future.

the power of communication and ideas flowing from the use of marketing's skills and knowledge can be a powerful catalyst for change

The power of system redesign

Every business is focused on exploiting or creating the new – innovation is its lifeblood. Everyday entrepreneurs raise millions to exploit new ideas and disruptive innovations. Billions are poured into R&D efforts to create new and better ways for people to achieve what they want. Even seemingly traditional businesses are constantly searching for faster, cheaper, better ways of doing things and exploiting new ideas. It is this creativity and inventiveness that is the engine room of our prosperity and increasing standards of living.

I believe that the future will be and will need to be characterised by innovation at the *system level*. The current system of consumption is unsustainable, so it stands to reason, those businesses and brands that will win will be those which can see and exploit system change. I'd like to outline two main areas where I believe that marketing and brands have a significant impact to make on the rebooting of our system. They are deliberately provocative and 'out there' in order to provoke a debate about our future direction of travel. If they make you think, then they've served their purpose.

Every business is social

Good versus goods.

Market-based, shareholder-capitalised businesses are not going anywhere – that is, in terms of their permanence and their prospects for never-ending growth. They are not going to miraculously disappear, to be replaced by social enterprises or cooperatives or any other new, more egalitarian structure. Winning, growing and making money are here to stay and will continue to be the engine of progress. The questions should be what progress do we want, how do we measure profit and how do we create businesses that are trusted to deliver against these expectations? I'm not arguing against social entrepreneurship, but, with most of the top economic entities in the world being corporations, there needs to be fundamental change in the way traditional businesses see their role, their responsibilities and assess their impact on the world.

The successful businesses and brands of the future, I believe, will adopt deliberate social aims that they will seek to achieve directly and powerfully through their business models. Social change will no longer be an inadvertent consequence of their activities, or a side activity, such as CSR, paid for by the business. There are many examples of businesses creating social capitalism already. eBay creates social capital by helping people understand that most people are trustworthy; Kiva and Zopa achieve enviable default rates on their loans by leveraging trust and social standing; Whipcar allows me to hire my car to complete strangers when I am not using it and means they don't need to buy a car.

These businesses are still mainly on the fringe, however, and, while big businesses, especially in difficult areas, are pouring more and more resources into sustainability and the like, they haven't figured out the bigger picture.

The change that I am talking about is very much in line with the 'cradle to cradle' thinking that was so brilliantly developed by William McDonough and Michael Braungart (2002) in their book of the same name. I think the concept of seeing the world as a closed system is powerful. This challenges us to design businesses, products and brands that can liberate resources to deliver a specific benefit, do good as they travel through the system, but then bring them back for re-use.

How can we redesign the system to bring us to a fundamentally more sustainable position? Walmart in the USA are putting huge effort into thinking about how they can move to a more sustainable place, exploring local supply chains and applying pressure on major suppliers to ensure sustainability. As consumer concern continues to grow, they will naturally move to deeper questions about how they can re-establish local production for local people while continuing to apply their advanced approaches to running an efficient retail empire. The supermarket business I want to use and invest in is the one that has a clearer, more compelling vision of their response to my changing needs and their changing responsibilities to protect me and my children's future.

System redesign could take so many paths and is such fertile territory for brands and their marketers. Go on, Nike – what about a social aim of tackling rising global obesity? Publish that in your annual report. McDonalds – why not teach families to cook healthy, nutritious food together in your restaurants, celebrating the local ingredients that you talk about so much? I'd be 'lovin'' it and, the next time I was in the mood for a burger, I might just be more inclined to tip the wink to your golden arches. Coca-Cola, why not invest in tackling the rising levels of teen depression through your social media, music initiatives and 'open happiness' positioning? British Gas – why not co-invest and finance the upgrading of heating boilers in all schools in the UK? It might not be as sexy as sponsoring two-time Olympic gold medal swimmer Rebecca Adlington, but it would deliver a much deeper social and environmental good.

This might sound like cause-related marketing, like turbo-charged CSR, but it goes deeper than that. It challenges the business from top to bottom to engineer its value chain not for maximum sales and profit but maximum contribution to the common good, directly as a result of the core business. This could be innovation, this could be the route to a different model.

this might sound like ... turbo-charged CSR, but it goes deeper than that

Selling less stuff

There is one last idea I find very provocative for business that I'd like to explore. The purpose of investments in marketing and brands that businesses make are primarily about getting us to buy, to stimulate demand and create an insatiable thirst for the new and exciting. David Taylor, of The BrandGym (www.brandgym.com), talks in his books and blogs about 'SMS – sell more stuff'. His point is that, often, the more strategic brand stuff can forget or get in the way of the core purpose of marketing, which is selling more stuff. David's blog and business is a fantastic view of current best practice in strategic branding and marketing.

I think the future of marketing, though, is in 'SLS – selling less stuff' and, along with this, destimulating demand and creating insatiable satisfaction with *now*. There is a serious crunch coming, caused by the rising global population and the rapidly expanding Chinese and Indian middle classes who aspire to a consumer lifestyle. We simply don't have enough resources to cope with the doubling of the demand for consumerism. I, for one, don't think we have any right to deny China and India, for example, their time consuming. What I think we need to do in the West is move over, move beyond consumption and be contented with consuming less.

the future of marketing, though, is in ... destimulating demand and creating insatiable satisfaction with *now*

So that means businesses need to start structuring their business models around this lesser demand and marketers need to change the record from buy, buy, buy to keep, keep, keep. This is exciting and terrifying; this needs massive innovation; this demands the highest levels of creativity. There will be many squares to be circled as these changes happen and it will require marketers to fundamentally reassess tools and techniques to achieve different outcomes.

marketers need to change the record from buy, buy, buy to keep, keep, keep

Choice is the key concept here. We need to provide and champion different choices for people and our customers. Brands and businesses need to provide different templates for feeling good over and above the drive for more consumption. This will require us to make moral and ethical choices on behalf of people. Marketing and advertising labours under the misapprehension that all we do is provide competitive choice for the consumer, who has a need and is going to fill it anyhow. I don't agree that this is the only effect of marketing and advertising, but, even if it were true, we mould and play on these needs. We magnify some elements and forget others. Marketing and advertising are not a blind cipher, just presenting different options. As Rory Sutherland said to me, 'All advertising is partly subliminal because it works on an emotional, unconscious level.' We need to choose what elements to highlight, what feelings to create and we need to be led by what we think is right, the social mission of our businesses, while listening hard to the various groups important to achieving balance.

Businesses – and that means the people working within them – need to raise their consciousness' about the choices they make from a moral perspective. This feels uncomfortable even to write – who are we to choose *for* people? The debate about behavioural economics has illuminated this struggle. Behavioural economics uses choice architecture – 'nudges' as Richard Thaler and Cass Sunstein (2008) call it – to push people down one path or another: it recognises the power of the default option. For example, if you want to make pension take-up higher, make the default opt-*in* as opposed to opt-*out*. The UK Government is about to pass this legislation. Every time a deliberate choice is made by a behavioural economist or marketer, however, the question is asked 'Why don't we just give people free choice?'

The bottom line is that we don't *have* free choice. Messaging, our economic model, marketing, business, advertising, innate human drives – all make it more likely that one outcome will win out over another. The weight of marketing and communications is focused on driving consumption and creating the need for more. John Grant, in his book *Co-opportunity* (2010), powerfully calls for a process of 'relocating the dreams' away from passive consumerism. We need to celebrate other things that create contentment away from just the thrill of consuming. John writes about reconnecting with nature, community, lifelong learning, play, social production and craft, citizenship and generativity. These are fertile ideas for a new product and marketing landscape.

Consuming is not the issue, however – it's how, what and how much we consume that makes the difference. As the malign effects of consumption manifest themselves more and more evidently through, for example, obesity, landfill, community collapse and rising temperatures, all of us, including our customers, will make different choices. We will look to business and their brands to provide a trustworthy vision of how, why and what to consume.

I think there will be three 'selling less stuff' principles that will emerge or are already doing so over the next decade in marketing. They are all elements of the future landscape of trust. Let's now take a look at them.

VALUING THE NOW

To state the obvious, the underlying tenet of most advertising and marketing is that you will be 'better' for having purchased this product or service. This creates the impetus to buy. When thrust in my direction thousands of times a week, millions of times a year, however, these messages leave the impression that we are all rather pathetic as we are and need to consume to make up for our inadequacies. This makes us feel discontented, therefore we need to buy.

The current economic situation is forcing people to reassess this consumption-driving process. Their reassessment is happening in an environment where mistrust is causing a whole raft of things to be questioned, from fat cat salaries to politicians' expenses. Changing attitudes to spirituality, the environment, models of success and friendship also have profound effects. Everything is now so connected that ideas, movements, changes, move faster and sweep more people up in them. We are all reassessing what makes us contented and many are coming to the conclusion that it isn't consumption that provides the answers. Personal debt is declining and there is a serious commitment to cutting fiscal deficits. Cuts are the order of the day and austerity is on everyone's lips. Those brands that help us to feel good about what we have now, command profitable relationships based on this and help

we are all reassessing what makes us contented and many are coming to the conclusion that it isn't consumption

us feel more contented with the choices we are faced with now will break through.

BUILT TO LAST, BUILT TO MOD

A few years ago, I blogged about my toaster – complaining about how I couldn't fix it when it broke. Within a few days, I received over 30 e-mails and comments from friends sharing my frustration (and also giving me advice on how to get into the thing!)

I never did fix my toaster, but it taught me something and led me on a journey that brings me joy every day: at the suggestion of some of my friends, I started to get into the 'modding' and 'meddling' community. 'Modding' and 'meddling' are the processes of changing, adapting and fixing everyday items to make them better. For example, my three-year-old HP laptop has black duct tape around one corner of the screen. At the back of my drawer is a bunch of old screens and roller balls for my beloved Blackberry Bold smartphone. Sugru (www.sugru.com) is my constant companion (see below). Both my laptop and phone suffered faults that, given their age, were not economic to repair, but, a few Internet searches and some time spent watching modding and meddling videos on YouTube gave me the confidence to attempt repairs myself. After some hairy moments, both are now working and I have developed a much more emotional bond with these pieces of cold electronic equipment. They are now truly mine because I've become part of their creation and life story. I feel empowered, I feel clever, I feel joy every time I look down and see the duct tape. I love the fact that I can take them apart and fix them. Try to get into an Apple iPhone, though, and you'll see that modding and meddling isn't part of the Apple mantra.

Will my behaviour become mainstream? Perhaps not, but people are becoming more and more tired of throwaway product designs. Successful services like Geek Squad are helping people to extend the life of tired equipment by ensuring that it is well-maintained and modular. ASUS **people are becoming more and more tired of throwaway product designs** computers design many of their laptops with the same modular design so that, if one component fails, a fix can be made. New products like Sugru, which is a mouldable silicone substance a bit like a permanent Blu-Tack, give new options to change and improve the design of products to suit you as an individual. Check out its website for fantastic examples of what people have done with a bit of time, a bit of Sugru and their own inventiveness.

In a world where people realise more about the impact of their consumption, their natural conclusion is to want things to last longer. Products and brands designed with this longevity, this modding and meddling in mind, will be those that I'll trust. The brand can either fight this or embrace the relationship profitably.

BUYING *RELATIONSHIPS* RATHER THAN *STUFF*

Increasing product quality and price competition over the past 20 years has delivered a market where people are trained into disloyalty. When every product works in a satisfactory fashion, most products look the same and price offers are abundant every day, why stick with one brand? We have trained people to believe that you get a better deal by shopping around. With greater access to information, greater price transparency and more conscious consumption, this belief might start to waiver.

This creates a great opportunity for brands to start to create propositions that are built on ongoing relationships rather than just blind, one-off consumption. The automotive sector has developed this relationship with a significant minority of their customers who get a new car every three years while paying a monthly charge. PC World, a computer retailer in the UK, is experimenting with a leasehire laptop model – you get a keenly priced laptop, paid for over a period, then it is replaced with a new model at a point in time. Apple, despite not embracing modding and meddling, has its Genius Bar concept for help, training and repairs to their equipment. These brands want to command a long-term relationship with their customers.

Greater consciousness about consumption will drive people to naturally ask questions about the credentials of the brands that they buy. Value equations are changing and are subject to longer-term analysis than previously. What is the point of buying a toaster that is unrepairable and will break immediately after the warranty ends? Now I can read about people's experiences live in the store on my phone through review sites *before* deciding on my purchase and make a different choice

Many of these ideas and new businesses models could be paid for by the efficiencies that trusted brands and the loyalty created, saving the cost of the current hugely inefficient marketing budgets. These resources could be reinvested in commanding and incentivising loyalty through new propositions, loyalty pricing and customisation. Instead of the marketing game being about gaming the consumer to constantly switch, the game becomes how to create and command loyalty over the lifetime of the relationship, which is both more efficient and more profitable for customer and producer.

many of these ideas and new businesses models could be paid for by the efficiencies that trusted brands and loyalty could create

This future is radical

This future is radical. Much of it won't play out this way or on the timescales presented, but change *is* afoot. There are just too many seismic shifts on the horizon for something big *not* to impact the way that we do things around here. The question I suppose is whether business will drive change or respond to it or do a bit of both.

The current level of respect for business is not tenable. There will be continued tension and suspicion that we will pay for in rising costs and falling revenues. That we need to rebuild trust in our brands and their reputation should not be debated. This problem may be patched with slight changes to products, marketing and the way that things are done. This may be highly likely in the short term, but it is my sincere hope that we take the opportunity to re-establish trust in our brands, our businesses and our marketing by driving radical change. Get out there and start doing.

Bibliography

Alexander, Jon (2010) Writings on Conservation Economy blog (at: www.conservation-economy.org).

Axelrod, Robert (1984) *The Evolution of Co-operation*. New York: Basic Books.

Bacharach, Michael and Gambetta, Diego (2001) 'Trust in signs', in Karen S. Cook (ed.), *Trust in Society*. New York: Russell Sage Foundation. pp. 148–184.

Bachmann, Reinhard and Zaheer, Akbar (eds) (2006) *Handbook of Trust Research*. Cheltenham UK: Edward Elgar.

Bains, Gurnek with Bains, Kylie and YSC team (2007) *Meaning Inc.: The blueprint for business success in the 21st century*. London: Profile Books.

Beck, Ulrich (1992) *Risk Society: Towards a new modernity*. London: Sage.

Blair, Tony (2010) *A Journey*. London: Hutchinson.

Creed, Douglas and Miles, Raymond (1996) 'Trust in organizations: A conceptual framework linking organizational forms, managerial philosophies, and the opportunity costs of controls', in M. R. Kramer and R. T. Tyler (eds), *Trust in Organizations: Frontiers of theory and research*. Thousand Oaks, CA: Sage. pp. 16–38.

Edelman (2010) '2010 Edelman trust barometer: An annual global opinion leaders study'. New York: Edelman Financial Services.

Fox, Alan (1974) *Beyond Contract: Work, power and trust relations*. London: Faber and Faber.

Fukuyama, Francis (1995) *Trust: The social virtues and the creation of prosperity*. New York: Free Press.

Gardner, Dan (2008) *Risk: The science and politics of fear*. London: Virgin Books.

Gerzema, John and Lebar, Ed (2008) *The Brand Bubble: The looming crisis in brand value and how to avoid it*. San Francisco, CA: Jossey-Bass.

Gilbreath, Bob (2010) *The Next Evolution of Marketing: Connect with your customers by marketing with meaning*. New York: McGraw-Hill.

Gladwell, Malcolm (2005) *Blink: The power of thinking without thinking*. New York: Little, Brown & Co.

Godin, Seth (2010) *Linchpin: Are you indispensable?* London: Piatkus.

Gordon, David S. and Platek, Steven M. (2009) 'Trustworthy? The brain knows: Implicit neural responses to faces that vary in dark triad personality characteristics and trustworthiness', *Journal of Social, Evolutionary, and Cultural Psychology*, 3 (3), pp. 182– 200.

Grant, John (2010) *Co-opportunity: Join up for a sustainable, resilient, prosperous world*. Chichester, West Sussex: John Wiley.

Hardin, Russell (2002) *Trust & Trustworthiness*. New York: Russell Sage Foundation.

Hulme, Michael (2010) 'Your brand: At risk or ready for growth?', May. Bristol: Alterian.

Institute of Leadership and Management (2010) 'Index of leadership trust 2010: The results'. Lichfield, Staffordshire: Institute of Leadership and Management.

Ipsos MORI (2009) 'Trust in doctors: Annual survey of public trust in professions', September. London: Royal College of Physicians.

Jacobs, Jane (1961) *The Death and Life of Great American Cities*. New York: Random House.

Johnson, Steven (2002) *Emergence: The connected lives of ants, brains, cities, and software*. New York: Touchstone.

Kahneman, Daniel and Tversky, Amos (1979) 'Prospect theory: An analysis of decision under risk', *Econometrica*, 47 (2), pp. 263–291.

Koehn, Nancy F. (2001) *Brand New: How entrepreneurs earned consumers' trust from Wedgwood to Dell*. Boston, MA: Harvard Business School Press.

Kohn, Marek (2008) *Trust: Self-interest and the common good*. Oxford: Oxford University Press.

Leakey, Richard (1994) *The Origin of Humankind: Unearthing our family tree*. London: Weidenfeld & Nicolson. p. 124.

LeGault, Michael R. (2006) *Think: Why crucial decisions can't be made in the blink of an eye*. New York: Threshold Editions.

Lévitt, Théodore (1960) 'Marketing myopia', *Harvard Business Review*, 38, pp. 24–47.

Marková, Ivana and Gillespie, Alex (eds) (2008) *Trust & Distrust: Sociocultural perspectives*. Charlotte, NC: Information Age Publishing.

Max-Neef, Manfred (1992) 'Development and human needs', in Paul Ekins and Manfred Max-Neef (eds), *Real-life Economics: Understanding wealth creation*. London: Routledge. pp. 197–213.

McDonough, William and Braungart, Michael (2002) *Cradle to Cradle: Remaking the way we make things*. New York: North Point Press.

Millward Brown (2010) 'Beyond trust: Engaging consumers in the post-recession world'. New York: Millward Brown and The Futures Company.

Mintel (2009) 'Mintel predicts global consumer trends for 2010'. Report and press
release, December. Mintel.

Read, Leonard E. (1999) 'I, Pencil: My family tree, as told to Leonard E. Read'.
Introduction by Milton Friedman. Irvington-on-Hudson, NY: The Foundation
for Economic Education.

Sacks, Oliver (1985) *The Man Who Mistook His Wife for a Hat*. London: Gerald
Duckworth.

Schwartz, Barry (2005) *The Paradox of Choice: Why more is less*. London:
HarperCollins.

Seldon, Anthony (2010) *Trust: How we lost it and how to get it back*. London:
Biteback.

Sennett, Richard (2006) *The Culture of the New Capitalism*. New Haven, CT and
London: Yale University Press.

Settle, Robert B. and Alreck, Pamela L. (1986) *Why They Buy: American consumers
inside and out*. Hoboken, NJ: John Wiley.

Sharp, Byron (2010) *How Brands Grow: What marketers don't know*. Oxford: Oxford
University Press.

Sigman, Aric (2005) *Remotely Controlled: How television is damaging our lives*.
London: Vermillion.

Six, Frédérique and Sorge, Andt (2008) 'Creating a high-trust organization: An
exploration into organizational policies that stimulate interpersonal trust
building', *Journal of Management Studies*, 45 (5), pp. 857–884.

Smith, Adam (1759) *The Theory of Moral Sentiments*. London: A. Millar.

Smith, Adam (1776) *An Inquiry into the Nature and Causes of the Wealth of Nations*.
London: W. Strahan & T. Cadell.

Sztompka, Piotr (1999) *Trust: A sociological theory*. Cambridge: Cambridge
University Press.

Thaler, Richard H. and Sunstein, Cass R. (2008) *Nudge: Improving decisions about
health, wealth, and happiness*. New Haven, CT: Yale University Press.

Todorov, Alexander, Mandisodza, Anesu N., Goren, Amir and Hall, Crystal C.
(2005) 'Inferences of competence from faces predict election outcomes',
Science, 10 June, 308 (5728), pp. 1623–1626.

Wright, Tom (2010) *Virtue Reborn*. London: Society for Promoting Christian
Knowledge.

Yamagishi, Toshio (2001) 'Trust as a form of social intelligence', in Karen S. Cook
(ed.), *Trust in Society*. New York: Russell Sage Foundation. pp. 121–147.

Index